Poor America

Poor America

A Comparative Historical Study of Poverty in the United States and Western Europe

Samuel J. Eldersveld

LEXINGTON BOOKS

A division of
ROWMAN & LITTLEFIELD PUBLISHERS, INC.
Lanham • Boulder • New York • Toronto • Plymouth, UK

LEXINGTON BOOKS

A division of Rowman & Littlefield Publishers, Inc.
A wholly owned subsidiary of The Rowman & Littlefield Publishing Group, Inc.
4501 Forbes Boulevard, Suite 200
Lanham, MD 20706

Estover Road
Plymouth PL6 7PY
United Kingdom

British Library Cataloguing in Publication Information Available

Library of Congress Cataloging-in-Publication Data

Eldersveld, Samuel James.
  Poor America : a comparative historical study of poverty in the United States and
Western Europe / Samuel J. Eldersveld.
    p. cm.
  Includes bibliographical references and index.
  ISBN-13: 978-0-7391-1163-5 (cloth : alk. paper)
  ISBN-10: 0-7391-1163-9 (cloth : alk. paper)
  1. Poverty—United States—History. 2. Economic assistance, Domestic—United
States. 3. Poverty—Europe, Western—History—Case studies. 4. Economic assistance,
Domestic—Europe, Western—Case studies. I. Title.
  HC110.P6E44 2007
  339.4'6094—dc22   2006033577

Printed in the United States of America

⊖™ The paper used in this publication meets the minimum requirements of American
National Standard for Information Sciences—Permanence of Paper for Printed Library
Materials, ANSI/NISO Z39.48–1992.

Dedicated to 37 million Americans living in poverty who deserve much better from their government.

Contents

List of Tables and Figures

Tables

Figures

Preface to Poor America

I wrote the final revisions and additions to this book in the midst of the presidential campaign of 2004 and finalized the writing in 2006. I find no political leaders discussing the extent of our poverty and none explicitly setting forth a plan to deal with it. Democratic candidate Edwards did refer to "the 35 million poor." But poverty these days is not a subject which Congress debates. Our national leaders ignore poverty—perhaps our greatest moral problem today.

And yet, the signs of poverty are all about us. The New York Times editorializes at length on how Bush's new budget penalizes the poor. And The Times often publishes a vignette on the "neediest cases" in the big city. And locally we see the evidence of pressure for shelters, free breakfasts for the destitute, and free dinners also, and the consequences of joblessness and inadequate assistance to the needy. The American conference of mayors reported that in its 25 largest cities there was in 2003 a 17% increase in shelter requests and a 14% increase in food requests—and half of these cities reported that they could not meet all these requests for help. The economy may be recovering but poverty has increased! Yet, where is evidence of elite concern?

The title of this book is "Poor America"—why? For several reasons. We have more poor in the United States today (37 million living below the poverty line) than is true proportionately in any other West European democracy. The title calls to our attention a particular group in our society which is relatively neglected. It is an expression of sympathy for them. It also expresses concern for our country which despite all its wealth and resources has fallen far behind other countries in Western Europe in benevolence and humane provision of poor relief. Perhaps it is also a statement of self-ridicule, but more than that it is a statement of astonishment. We are truly degraded.

How did I come to write a book like this? In recent years I have often been on trips to countries like the Netherlands and Sweden and discussed with business leaders and intellectuals their virtual elimination of poverty. It is always an embarrassing experience. But my concern goes far back to earlier years. In part it was a result of my perceptions and feelings as a young boy growing up in the Depression as one of seven children in a poor religious family where my father, a minister, always sternly reminded us that if a poor person came to our door (as they often did) we should never send them away without something to eat. In part it goes back further to the story of my father's family being so poor in the Netherlands that he and his sister, age 16 and 18 were given the family's savings for passage to America. He found a job in a shoe factory in Chicago and sent his savings home so that all his family including his father and mother could come to Chicago. It is ironic that he did so well in "wonderful America!" But my experiences as I worked toward a university education sharpened my perceptions and concerns. I must admit also that my sortie into local politics in Ann Arbor, including being elected as mayor, opened up to me better than ever an awareness of how even in an affluent city like Ann Arbor (in 1957) there were plenty of marginalized citizens here who felt quite free to call up the mayor day or night to explain their plight. Thus, a combination of experiences led to my preoccupation with the problem of poverty in America.

One may question the wisdom of a book like this at this time. A nation deep in war and deficit and a declining dollar, and with so many economic and social problems—one could say this is not the time to discuss poverty. Yet it is an issue we must face eventually. We should have faced it long ago. For a modernized, developing democracy it is a condition which challenges us. True it will cost many billions of dollars. But all of Western Europe spent heavily also long ago to eliminate poverty and do so still today. If we care to be seen as a humane society, an anti-poverty program is essential.

In recent years several books have been published on poverty. In 2004 Geoffry Gilbert published World Poverty providing data on the extent and variations of poverty in the world. He argues for ways to reduce poverty. Jeffrey Sach's The End of Poverty (2006) describes the policies and millions of funding by nations which are necessary to end poverty. These and other studies are useful. In these studies and others no one does a truly comparative study of the history of poverty in nations and includes the success of these comparative approaches to the solution of poverty.

The plan of the book is quite simple. It starts off in chapter 1 presenting the data on poverty for the United States and six European countries. The focus of the book is to explain as far as possible why the variance, why these West European countries have successfully dealt with poverty while we have not. Chapters 2 through 6 examine the different theories which have been advanced to explain this variance, or difference, between the United States and Europe. In the latter part of the book there is a lengthy historical description and analysis of the way each of these seven countries have dealt with poverty. The last section presents a final report of the 20th century reform legislation, particularly after World War II, and how it differed from the post war American experience.

This study, it should be emphasized, has the focus on poverty as one way to understand the condition of the poor. Poverty is defined as the portion of the population which lives at or below 40% —42% of the median family income in the United States and other nations. Each nation in a sense has a "poverty line" which is the level of income needed for an individual or for a family to meet basic needs.

My purpose here is not to determine whether this is adequate for living and personal needs such as housing, education, food, health or other particular benefits. Nor is it my intention to provide specific explanations of the factors responsible. Other scholars have discussed this in depth. Poverty obviously is the result of the incapacity of the system in a variety of ways to take care of the needy. I am interested in the total burden of poverty in the United States and the Western European systems and how these systems vary in their concern and capability in dealing with such problems.

It is interesting that poverty centers in the United States have been studying these questions such as the poverty center at the University of Michigan. New centers have been created recently, such as the poverty center at the University of North Carolina by former Senator John Edwards and the University of California has created one at Berkeley.

In reading the book one should keep in mind at what level of society the analysis is made. This is basically a study of the leaders, the elites of these seven countries and the decisions they made as to how to deal with the poverty problem in their system. These decisions by the institutional elites is the focus here although public attitudes are evaluated and were data are available, public opinion values and attitudes are analyzed (see Chapter 3 for the United States).

The ideas of new governmental leaders, business elites, attitudes towards the role of poverty and dealing with poverty are also presented when such data are available (Chapter 6).

The book attempts to present both the empirical and qualitative evidence, which is available, from our studies in each of these countries. There is a great deal of literature on the subject of poverty in the United States and Europe. But no one has really attempted a systematic comparative—historical study focused on the explanation of why we in the United States have not successfully dealt with the problem of poor relief as well as the West Europeans have. Once we understand this, hopefully we may be able in America to identify the approach needed to solve the poor relief problem on a national level.

Many friends provided assistance to me in this project—accessing materials, recommending studies, helping with translations, evaluating my interpretations, and suggesting revisions. The final product was my responsibility, but completion would have been difficult without their help. I am particularly grateful to: Professor Frits L. Van Holthoon, University of Groningen, the Netherlands, Professor Eric Ketelaar, University of Amsterdam, the Netherlands, Dr. Ton Broos, University of Michigan, US, Professor Hugh Bochel, University of Humberside, England, Dr. Hugo and Karla Von der Sypen, University of Michigan, US, Klaus Liepelt, research scholar, Germany, Jean Marie and Miems Duléry, Paris, France, Professor Lucy E. Murphy (daughter), Ohio State University, US, Professor Judith Kullberg, Eastern Michigan University, US, Dr. J.L. Vrooman, research scholar, Social Welfare Ministry, The Hague, the Netherlands, Dr. Marijke W. de Kleijn-de Vrankrijker, research scholar, Leiden, the Netherlands, Paul Van den Muysenberg, former Dutch consul, Detroit, US, Professor Mary Corcoran, University of Michigan Poverty Center, School of Public Policy, US. I am particularly indebted to my able secretary, Holly Bender. I am grateful to all these friends.

Above all I want to express my gratitude to my wife, Dr. Els Nieuwenhuijsen and my son, Dr. Samuel K. Eldersveld without whose help the final version could not be completed.

Samuel J. Eldersveld
May 21, 2006
Ann Arbor, Michigan. U.S.A.

Part I

The State of Poverty in the United States and Western Europe: Five Theoretical Approaches Seeking to Explain the Variance

Chapter 1

The Challenge to America: The State of Poor Relief in Western Europe and the United States

The true test of the humaneness of a group, or society, or nation is how it cares for its poorest members. One may argue for other tests, for other sectors of the population or other attributes (liberty, equality, health, justice, etc.). But in the last analysis we are judged by how well we, the public and the elites, respond to the basic subsistence needs of the impoverished, the destitute, the indigent, and the disadvantaged. How well we accept this fundamental moral responsibility distinguishes societies, exalts them in world regard or lowers them in world regard. This depends of course on one's ultimate values. If a nation's elites value the accumulation of wealth per se, or economic power, or military brilliance, then the humaneness of the system will be belittled. But in a democracy, particularly, a great nation should never try to escape its obligation to its impoverished masses.

If one studies the histories of nations one soon comes to a realization that each country over time develops a particular way of thinking about poverty—its causes, its characteristic manifestations, its effects on society, its meaning for the individual person and his or her family. Similarly in each country a way of acting toward poverty emerges, a set of conceptions about how to deal with it, how most effectively to provide poor relief. Above all, one senses that in each country there does or does not emerge a sense of societal and governmental responsibility for dealing with poverty, a responsibility felt by the public but above all by its political, intellectual, social, and business elites. If this sense of responsibility is absent, or not persistent, or not fully embraced that system will, in terms of its humaneness, be degraded.

One challenging puzzle of modern democracies is the variation in their

provision for the poor. Why is it that the governing elites in the United
States after all these years apparently seem incapable and/or unwilling to
solve the problem of poverty while most Western European elites have done
a better job? This is all the more difficult to accept because of the economic power and resources of the American system. Presumably we are
the affluent society. Periodically in the Twentieth Century we sought to
provide salvation to the poor. President F.D. Roosevelt's New Deal certainly struggled long and hard, adopting a variety of programs, from the
"dole" to Works Project Administration (WPA)—a government paid work
program to help the poor maintain themselves until most of them went to
work in World War II. And other presidents have also sought to deal with
the problem of the poor—Truman with his Full Employment Act, Johnson
with his War on Poverty, and most recently in 1996 Clinton's PRWORA
(Personal Responsibility and Work Opportunities Reconciliation Act). Yet
today we are still asking each other what should we do, how should we
correct the inadequacies and shortcomings of the 1996 legislation? After
over 200 years of arguing publicly over what our system should do, after
hundreds of books, studies, analyses and reports on poverty we are still at a
point where conditions are worsening rather than being resolved. We have
millions living below the "poverty line" while in Western Europe there are
indeed poor people, but a much smaller percentage of the population lives
below the poverty line. There are few ghettos or slums in Western Europe
such as we have in the United States. Why is this? In newspapers and
on televisions virtually every week we see references to poverty throughout
the United States. For example, recently the well-known talk show hostess
Oprah Winfrey interviewed homeless people on television in San Francisco
and conducted the program by asking the question: "What kind of America
do we want?"

The latest report of the U.S. Census Bureau on the status of poverty
covers the year 2004. The proportion of Americans living below the poverty
line was 12.7%. Which is 37 million persons.[1]

This was an increase from 11.3% in 2000. The number in poverty has
increased by over four million since 2000. These numbers are disturbing.
Despite all our efforts (lately under the 1996 law) the poverty rate is unac-
ceptably high.

Overtime Data on American Poverty

Our latest figure of 12.7% poverty for households for the year 2004 should
be compared to the previous 40 years to see whether we have done better
or worse (see Table 1.1).
Professor Mary Corcoran of the Poverty Center of the University of Michi-

gan identifies a zig-zag pattern of poverty, decline and increase over a long period of time, but never lower than 10%. It is clear that the percentage of poverty varied a great deal over time. In part there is a pattern of ups and downs. Here are the different patterns:

1949–1973	Sharp digs in poverty
1973–1981	Big jump in poverty
1981–1988	The Reagan period resulted in a small reduction in poverty
1989–1992	The poverty rate increased
1993–2001	Policy changes and earned income tax credit (EITC) results in a lower poverty rate
2001–2004	Increase in the poverty rate to 12.7%

Table 1.1: Change in the United States Poverty Rates Over Time

Year	Level of Poverty in Percentage
1968 –	12.8
1974 –	11.2
1986 –	13.6
1997 –	13.3
2004 –	12.7

These variations were caused by changes in governmental policy and by changes in economic development.

One must also remember the considerable disparity in poverty rates for population subgroups. Some examples for 2004 are[2]:

Non-Hispanic Whites	8.6% of total white population
Non-Hispanic Blacks	24.7% of the total black population
Hispanics	21.9% of the total Hispanic population

Variations in Poverty by Types of Families:	
children under 18	14.3%
single-gender parent	37.2%
black, with children under 18	28.1%
black, single-gender parent	45.0%
Hispanic, single-gender parent	45.1%

Obviously, there are family groups in our population who are suffering severely.

One must keep in mind that of the total population of people in poverty 45% are white, 25% are black and 24% are Hispanic Americans. Thus, those living below the poverty line represent most ethnic groups. In actuality, the rate of poverty in most American cities is over 20%.[3]

These developments of poverty are associated with other changes in the American population. The increase in enequality of income is one characteristic of the development. The gap between rich and poor is greater and at its highest level in two decades. In 2004, the poorest fifth of the population received 3.4% of the total household income, while the wealthiest fifth of the population received 51% of the household income (compared to 4.0% in 1985 for the poorest fifth and 45% for the richest fifth.)[4] Greater inequality today than before! Our hope after the passage of the 1996 Act (the "Welfare to Work Law") was for some real amelioration of poverty. The poverty rate did drop from 13.7% in 1996 to 11.3% in 2000. But poverty began increasing again in 2001 and was 12.7% in 2004. The big point is that our pattern of national poverty changed over time, dependent on presidential policies and economic currents. But poverty persists, and remains high—37 million people were poor in 2004. Thus, the key question remains; is this acceptable for the richest country in the world? This figure today is very similar to the poverty level in the mid 1960's. This suggests that there has been no change over time. But in reality this is not true. Poverty has fluctuated considerably.

The 1990s economic boom and welfare reform decade was accompanied by lower poverty levels. More than one in ten Americans and one in seven American children were poor at the end of the decade. The 1990 reforms may have gotten people off welfare, but put many of them into jobs which did not get them out of poverty. We have a major problem with the plight of the "working poor." Poverty persists in America.

The 1996 Law and Proposals for Revision

The current law adopted in 1996 is called the Personal Responsibility and Work Opportunity Reconciliation Act (PRWORA). One of its functions is called TANF (Temporary Assistance for Needy Families). Under this Act the care for the poor is very decentralized in the United States today. It has two leading characteristics. The first is that states will be provided a certain amount of money from the federal government which, subject to certain requirements, each state has great flexibility to administer. Thus the actual poverty program in each state will be unique and, in a sense, experimental. The pattern and extent of assistance to the poor is thus very diverse at the local level. The second principle is that welfare rolls must be reduced, while also demanding that most people on welfare must be working. The long term goal is to get people off welfare and into jobs, at which time they may or may not be assisted by the state to reach the poverty threshold.

The assumptions implicit in this Act are that the provision for the poor has to be handled differently by state, and that getting people off welfare will reduce poverty. Both assumptions are seriously questioned. The only specifications which all states must meet are (1) that individuals can not be on welfare for more than five years, (2) that 50% of those on welfare must hold jobs, and (3) that 50% of the states' case load must be working 30 hours per week. States not meeting these requirements are subject to financial penalties, as are families who do not meet work requirements. The government allocates each year $16.9 billion to be distributed to the states.

This legislation was considered effective by some because of the reduction of persons on welfare. On average the states reported a 50% reduction. This is cited as evidence of success. There was a decline over time in the national poverty rate, but that increased again to 12.7%. The concerns over the criteria for the operation of the 1996 Act are many, discussed in detail by several scholars.[5] Since the adoption of the 1996 Act, the extension of the Act in subsequent years has been delayed. This is due to controversies between the two parties on the amount of work required as well as on the promises for child caring services. The 1996 Act was renewed in February 2006. The 1996 Act as administered by the states "seems to have helped some families gain a foothold in the labor market. . . . for other families, the story is less clear. Some families who are no longer receiving welfare are not working and report little or no income."[6] Although there is obviously some progress, "it is clear that the transformation of the safety net is far from complete." Above all, once we found ourselves in a recession, poverty is again on the rise.

A Comparison of American and European Poverty Levels

If we compare United States poverty rates with those of Western Europe any time in the post war period we find persistent evidence that the United States is less generous, less humane, less concerned and less interested in providing for all of the poor than any of these other modern democracies. Many scholars have written on this subject and calculated the comparative data. A perfect comparative measure is probably not possible. But the most common measure defines those in poverty as the percent of the population with 40% or less of the median household income in a country. This comes closest to the United States poverty line estimates which are now about 42% of median household income. If we use this measure we arrive at the poverty rates found in Table 1.2

More recent data compiled by the Luxembourg Income Study (LIS)[7] demonstrate for later years the striking contrast between West European countries and the United States. Similar data are presented by Smeeding,

Table 1.2: Comparative Poverty Rates—United States and Western Europe Before 2000

	U.S.	Ger-many*	France	Bel-gium	UK	Nether-lands	Sweden
Year	1997	1994	1994	1992	1995	1994	1995
Overall Rate	10.7	4.2	3.2	1.9	5.7	4.7	4.6
Children's Rate	14.7	6.0	2.6	1.6	8.3	4.6	1.3

Source: Sheldon Danziger and Robert H. Haveman, *Understanding Poverty*, Harvard: Russell Sage, 2001, p. 173. *German data include East Germany.

Table 1.3: Comparative Poverty Rates. United States and Western Europe After 2000

	U.S.	Bel-gium	France*	Ger-many	Nether-lands	Sweden	UK
Year	2000	2000	1994	2000	1999	2000	1999
Overall Rate	10.8	3.7	3.4	4.7	4.6	3.8	5.8
Children's Rate	14.1	3.8	2.9	5.8	5.8	1.8	5.5

*Later data from France are not yet available. Source: Luxembourg Income Study (LIS) file 2006

but he uses the 50% median adjusted disposable income for individuals.[8] Tables 1.2 and 1.3 summarize our findings before and after 2000 except for France for which the most recent data are not available.

Tables 1.4 and 1.5 are particularly significant because the data reveals how little relatively, the United States policies have reduced poverty in the United States compared to reductions in Western European countries.[9] It is clear from these tables that the United States has twice as much poverty (with the exception of the UK) and child poverty is three times higher than in West Europe, except for UK and Germany. After 2000 the data reveal a striking contrast between the U.S. and Western European countries. Other studies by the European Union or by scholars in Western Europe produce very similar data.[10]

It is important to realize that these figures (above) are the percentage of persons with an income below the poverty "line" or "threshold." A secondary concern is called "closing the gap" between those with low poverty income levels and a decent minimal standard of living (the poverty threshold), by providing assistance to the poor beyond their low poverty incomes. The West European countries do this to a much greater extent than the

Table 1.4: The Differential in Poverty Rates Between the United States and West European Nations based on Table 1.3

	Bel-gium	France*	Ger-many	Nether-lands	Sweden	UK
United States comparison at 40% level	+7.1	(+7.4)	+6.1	+6.2	+7.0	+5.0
United States comparison at median income 40% level on children	+10.3	(+11.2)	+8.3	+8.3	+12.3	+8.6

*Later data on France are not yet available Source: Luxembourg Income Study (LIS) file 2006.

United States, on the basis of available studies.[11,12] The United States pays some subsistence benefits to close the gap under our SSI law (Supplemental Security Income Act) but it does not come close to "closing the gap."

Linked to these differences are the allocations by government for social welfare generally in these countries. The percent of GDP allocated for social welfare expenditures varies considerably — in 1998 it was 18.0% for the United States, but close to or over 30% for Western Europe (e.g. 32.9% for France, 34.5% for Sweden, 26.9% for the Netherlands).[13] The United States persistently lags behind these European states in its provision for social relief. Why is this? This puzzle has confronted many scholars over the years. This incapacity or unwillingness of the Untied States to cope with the poverty problem at the same level as those in Europe has never had a complete and convincing explanation. In a country like the Netherlands, for example, long ago the government forthrightly addressed this poverty problem, and passed a law in 1965 called the General Assistance Law (*Algemene Bijstandswet*) in which the national parliament declared that all "subjects" (members of the public) "as a matter of right" should be provided a decent standard of living. The government assumed basic responsibility to see that each and every person would have the basic "social minimum" of needs met, regardless of condition. While this has not wiped out poverty completely but has reduced it dramatically. It is truly difficult to understand why the United States has never really accepted this sense of responsibility.

Table 1.5: Comparative Data on Reduction of Poverty: the Percent Reduction of Poverty due to State Actions

	U.S.	Bel-gium	France	Ger-many	Nether-lands	Sweden	UK
Year	2000	2000	–	2000	1999	2000	1999
% reduction of poverty due to state policy actions	26.4	76.9	–	70.5	65.2	77.4	60.1

Source: Smeeding 2006 page 79.

This comparative shortcoming of the United States system is embarrassing to an American citizen—it is difficult to accept. The United States is an economic power and has more financial capability than each of these Western European systems. For example, per capita GDP income for the United States in 1998 was $32,184 while all of the Western European systems were much lower–an average of $21,950 (Germany was highest with $23,010).[14] This makes it difficult to accept the unwillingness of the American political elites to eliminate poverty. Second, we have had a long belief as a nation in equality, although the meaning of it and the actual existence of it, have been questioned over the years. De Toqueville stated that he was impressed with the American "equality of condition."[15] Others have denied that even in De Toqueville's day (mid 19th century) that was true.[16] Still others argue that the old equalitarian tradition changed subsequently to equality of opportunity, has been lost, despite the efforts of the Progressives, the New Dealers, and the Great Society believers. The modern capitalists and the conservative right have so effectively argued for individual liberty that programs to focus on the values of economic redistribution and even equality of opportunity have lost out. But the battle for economic justice still confronts us and "if it is to survive a truly democratic government of the people requires a fundamental equality and justice in the distribution of wealth."[17]

Our history attests to the clashes of opinions over economic inequality. As Sean Wilentz describes it, inequality was relatively low during the Colonial and Revolutionary periods (excluding Indians and slaves). During the Jefferson period and into the 19th century equality was a value most leaders subscribed to. The transformation of American society after 1815 with the onset of the industrial revolution and market capitalism, inequality increased, and also poverty. "The richest one percent held nearly 30% of the nation's wealth" by 1860. Political conflict between the Jackson Democrats and the Whigs over the wealth and monopolistic power of the "aristocrats" before the Civil War was followed by the conflicts between the "new" Republicans and the Democrats in the Reconstruction following the War. The rise of great new corporations led to the questioning of "equalitarian assumptions." By the 1920s "gross inequality now turned out to be a perfectly natural result of market forces." From then on the conflict between the older equalitarian concept was opposed by the new apology for big business and market capitalism.[18]

Explanations and Theories

The primary question here is why the variance between the United States and Western European countries in dealing with poverty. Why, after all these years, has the United States failed to follow the English and West European example, why have we not enacted a basic anti-poverty law committing the national government to providing to all Americans the guarantee of a descent standard of living what the Europeans call the "social minimum"? Many scholars have advanced explanations and theories addressed to this question. These interpretations are often controversial. In our analysis we will focus on five approaches searching for answers. These are: 1. The historical argument, what is the relevance of historical experience for understanding how these nations in recent years have responded to the poverty problem. Has this historical experience socialized European publics and elites to support a different solution to the poverty problem than the historical experience of the United States has socialized American elites and its public? 2. The political system approach. Have the political institutions and process in the United States been so different from those in West Europe, particularly because of the distribution of power and the complexity of the decision making process in the United States, that legislation on poverty has been difficult (if not impossible) in the United States compared to Europe? 3. The values approach. Have the values, beliefs, and attitudes of European publics developed in such a way overtime that a public consensus was achieved in Western Europe in support of comprehensive poor relief, while this consensus has never been achieved in the United States, thus precluding such governmental action in the United Sates? 4. The political elite system approach. Are the types of political leaders who hold high office basically different in the United States compared to Europe—in their social backgrounds, in their access to public office (i.e. in their recruitment opportunities), in their relationships to their constituents, and in their predispositions in favor of benevolent governmental action providing poor relief—are these characteristics of the elite systems so different that they comprise an adequate explanation for American failure? 5. The business elite's role in the system. The question has for long been raised—are the American corporate and business elites much more opposed to poor relief than in Europe, and do they play a much more significant role in the policy process than in Europe, thus constituting a basic "block" to anti-poverty legislation? In short, does American free-market capitalism turn out to be less humane, less interested in social reform, than is the case with European free-market capitalism?

We will analyze and explain in succeeding chapters these causal theories, adducing what evidence we can find to arrive at preliminary answers to the questions posed.

Notes

1. U.S. Census Bureau. *Historical Poverty Tables.*
http://www.census.gov/hhes/www/poverty/histpov/hstpov2.html (accessed August 21, 2006)

2. Sheldon H. Danziger and Robert H. Haveman eds., Understanding Poverty, (Cambridge, MA: Harvard University Press, 2001), 101, 124–5.

3. Bernstein, Jared. Who's Poor? Don't Ask the Census Bureau. Why the Current Measure of Poverty used by the Census Bureau is Obsolete. *New York Times*, 26 Sept. 2003, 25.

4. U.S. Census Bureau. *Historical Poverty Tables.*

5. See for example, Danziger and Haveman, *Understanding Poverty*, 230-276.

6. Danziger and Haveman, *Understanding Poverty*, 233.

7. Luxembourg Income Study (LIS) File of 31 January 2006. Relative Poverty Rates for the Total Population. Children and the Elderly http://www.lisproject.org/keyfigures/povertytable.htm (accessed August 21, 2006).

8. Timothy Smeeding, "Poor People in Rich Nations: The United States in Comparative Perspective". *Journal of Economic Perspectives* 20, no.1 (Winter 2006): 69-90.

9. Smeeding, "Poor People in Rich Nations"

10. See for example J.M.W. Schut, J.C. Vrooman, T. de Beer, *On Worlds of Welfare: Institutions and their Effects on Eleven Welfare States.* Social and Cultural Planning Office of the Netherlands (The Hague, the Netherlands: Planning Office, 2001), 125.

11. Danziger and Haveman, *Understanding Poverty*, 2001, 162-189; see also Cristina Behrendt, *At the Margins of the Welfare State*, 2002, (Aldershot, England: Ashgate Publishers), 38–42.S

12. Danziger and Haveman, *Understanding Poverty*, 178.

13. Sheldon H. Danziger, Gary D. Sandefur and Daniel H. Weinberg, eds, *Confronting Poverty: Prescriptions for change*, (Cambridge, MA.: Harvard), 1994, 81. The 1995 data are from the Organization for Economic Cooperation and Development (OECD), Social Expenditure Data.

14. These data are cited in Christopher Jencks, "Does Inequality Matter?",

Daedalus: Journal of the American Academy of Arts and Sciences, 131, no. 1 (Winter 2002), 54.

15. Alexis de Tocqueville, *Democracy in America*, (New York: Knopf, 1945).

16. Sidney Verba, *Elites and the Idea of Equality*, (Cambridge, Mass.: Harvard 1987), 43.

17. Sean Wilentz, "America's lost equalitarian tradition", Daedalus: Journal of the American Academy of Arts and Sciences, 131, no. 1, (Winter 2002), 66-80.

18. Sean Wilentz, "America's lost equalitarian tradition", 77.

Chapter 2

The Historical Experience as a Partial Explanation

In describing and comparing the history of these seven countries in their efforts to deal with poverty one must keep in mind their differences, as well as similarities. Obviously these countries differ in the magnitude of their poverty, their resources to deal with it, the role of local and national leaders, the role of the church, and to some extent, the public pressure to deal with poverty. In this first historic chapter on the United States we shall describe these conditions going back to early colonial days. In later chapters we will keep this in mind in our comparative observations. But the specific historic details will be found.

Of all the causal theories the historical approach can be the most controversial. This is because much of the evidence is not available. One must depend on "snapshots" provided by historical scholars, and if one wishes to demonstrate a linkage between early history and modern developments, as we do, the linkage is often arguable. In the last half of this book we have presented special chapters describing in detail the early history, and more contemporary history, of poverty and its relief in seven different countries. We draw on those analyses here in summarizing our findings, from which we seek to present a series of interpretations comparing the United States to West European countries.

The great deal of time we have spent on historical scholarship on the poverty question has been very useful. Such a study reveals how each society sought to respond to, and cope with, the problems of the poor. This throws much light on whether, and how nations in the late 19th century and early 20th century moved toward social reforms which eventually led to the modern society's resolution of the poverty question. We do not want to suggest here that there was a clear and simple path from the past to the present. The more we study the histories of these countries we realize

15

that different scenarios emerged. In fact we find that for no country was there a perfect "connect" between what happened in the earlier centuries and later.

The study of poverty in the earlier centuries (15th through the 18th) reveals similar conditions. There was a great deal of poverty, rising to over 50% of the population at times. But it was episodic, fluctuating because of poor harvests, epidemics, wars, taxation policies, etc. The care of the poor was local. In the early days it was communal, with churches, charities, the local wealthy, and families attempting to cope. Gradually poor relief became better organized, with local governments assuming a great deal of the burden. In England under the 1601 Elizabethan Poor Law the parishes were responsible for their poor, in France the local Catholic church. In Sweden it was communal and familial, as 95% of the people lived in rural areas surviving under very harsh conditions. In the Netherlands, city governments took control, assigning "overseers of the poor" to supervise the poor in their district, along with the local Reformed church in the area. Often the city council assumed control, adopting a poor tax, approaching wealthy benefactors, soliciting for contributions house to house. In the American colonies, studies of Boston, New York, and Philadelphia describe in detail the state of poverty and the elaborate organization set up to provide poor relief. There was a real sense of commitment in the 18th century colonies to care for the poor, with ingenious approaches experimented with to provide both "outdoor" and "indoor" (almshouses, work houses, even farm "colonies") to help the poor, relief which was usually but not always, benevolent and available usually, but not always, to all the poor. In the early days there was not as much evidence of distinguishing between the "worthy" and "unworthy" poor as developed later in the 18th and 19th centuries.

The historical process which followed this early period could be interpreted as of three types, at least: (1) early approaches which seemed to be relatively benevolent, followed by more harsh legislative actions, which in turn were completely reversed and overturned in the 20th century. (England may be a case in point). Considerable ideological argument could be involved in these historical "switches" in approach. (2) A persistent pattern of rather benevolent care for the poor with periodic debates over whether the local government (and the churches) or national government should assume responsibility, the national government eventually taking over this "public function" in the 20th century (the Netherlands perhaps is illustrative). (3) Only local communal and familial charity until the 20th century when the national government takes control as part of a broad gauged social reform program (Sweden may be an example of this). However, one must add to this discourse at once that each system had its own historical path. As one reads these histories one senses that there is a sort of historical experimentation taking place in each society moving from fairly simple to more complex approaches, mixed with much debate, study, publication of reports, support and condemnation of various schemes and strategies. Differing "poverty cultures" developed, revised from time to time in their conception of poverty, its causes, and its consequences, as well as what the proper task of government is in helping the poor. And all of these countries with their conflicting experiences, alternating approaches, more or less concerned about the poverty problem (and more or less in despair about it)—were converging on the 20th century, having to come to grips eventually with poverty and trying to craft their own solution to it.

For us in this research the big question is: in what way, if any, was the United States different from the Western European countries, including England, and how might this help to explain the different approach to poverty in the United States? The argument in the following pages which attempts to distinguish the American historical pattern from the West European has the following structure. While in all of these countries poverty was an early concern, indeed a major concern, and dealt with at the local level of these systems, by a variety of familial, religious, charitable, and local governing bodies, over time certain major distinctions can be described. These were:

Yet, while all of this seems noncomparable, even a bit idiosyncratic, history no doubt played a significant role. The increasing seriousness of poverty became a deep concern, the content of ideological arguments was well known, the success and failure of certain "experiments" to help the poor were quite evident, and a national (popular and elite) consciousness of the "public-ness" of the problem became deeply, or shallowly, imbedded in persons' minds. The historical process in each country in a sense laid the groundwork for a society eventually fashioning its basic way of responding to its needy. Each country thus was a four to five century "case study" in motion, "trying out" its ideas on how to deal with the poor. And in each country its citizens were undergoing a "socialization experience", in the aggregate, learning from its handling of poverty, what was successful and what failed, what was possible and what impossible, what was wrong and what was right.

For us in this research the big question is: in what way, if any, was the United States different from the Western European countries, including England, and how might this help to explain the different approach to poverty in the United States? The argument in the following pages which attempts to distinguish the American historical pattern from the West European has the following structure. While in all of these countries poverty was an early concern, indeed a major concern, and dealt with at the local level of these systems, by a variety of familial, religious, charitable, and local governing bodies, over time certain major distinctions can be described. These were:

1. The gradual awareness, even historically late, that the poor were citizens worthy of support, and that poor relief should not be organized on the assumption that some poor were worthy and some unworthy of relief. The Europeans got over that invidious dichotomy eventually; in a sense the United States never has, completely.

2. West European countries accepted the position that care for the poor was a public function and a public responsibility. While during the

colonial period city councils did what they could to alleviate poverty, there was an interruption in this sense of commitment in the 19th century and a desire (even today) to rely heavily on private charity.

3. The European countries finally accepted national public responsibility for caring for all the poor, and adopted legislation based on that belief. In the United States we have yet to admit to such a principle, struggling in the meantime with partial efforts to care for the poor while urging our charities on to assume a greater role.

We will elaborate each of these basic "differences" in our presentation to follow. In the review of the history of Western European countries one notices that the national (central) government relatively early, played a role by taking the initiative, or by seeking to take the initiative, in providing poor relief. The early efforts at social welfare reform were often relevant for poor relief. Germany of course is the most obvious immediate example with Bismarck's reform programs of the 1880s. In the Netherlands, once the seven provinces of the "low countries" were united, there was evidence of a national level interest. The 1798 constitution declares alleviation of poverty as a state responsibility, and King Willem I added his commitment to that. As we know there was a major argument in the 1850s on whether the national or local authorities should provide poor relief. Parliament awarded a major role to the local authorities and churches, which lasted until the national government adopted the Poor Law of 1912.

In the other countries the national government also usually played a major role. In England the Elizabethan Poor Law was adopted already in 1601 spelling out precisely that the parishes were to provide for the poor. In a sense this lasted until the Poor Law of 1834, harshly criticized by the liberals. After the Royal Commission appointed in 1905 reviewed and evaluated it, it was again revised and replaced by a new law adopted by Parliament in 1909. In France the Revolution in 1789 changed radically the administration of poor relief when the Constitutional Committee asserted it was a national responsibility, and for a time took over this public function from the Catholic Church. Later, Napoleon welcomed the Catholic Church back to a resumption of its major role in caring for the needy, but it was made clear that the national government in Paris would supervise and control the administration of poor relief by local authorities and the church. In the latter part of the 19th century the French national Parliament adopted a series of welfare laws, beginning in 1893 with a provision of free medical aid for the poor.

Even in Belgium before its independence in 1830 there was considerable debate over who should be in charge of the poverty relief program. Emperor Joseph actually decreed that a new system of charity would be set up and administered by the central state. When the emperor left, the system reverted to local officials and the local Catholic Church again. Yet, the argument continued and later in the 19th century, in 1889, the government in Brussels introduced its first social welfare legislation. Finally, in the case of Sweden there is the least evidence of an early role of the national government, preoccupied as it was with its many wars of aggression and defense. Sweden remained 75% to 80% rural until late in the 19th century, and relief was provided by families and villagers and small towns. As the industrial revolution came to Sweden late, from the 1870s, the political and social conflicts in the parliament of this constitutional monarchy, combined with mass level protests, and the rise of socialism, led to national legislation efforts to adopt social reforms, leading to their first old age pension law in 1913. Thus, in all these West European countries, either before or during the 19th century, there was an assumption of a national role in poor relief. This was not true in the United States.

This contrast between the United States and West Europe historically is significant. Our national government in Philadelphia or Washington revealed no great interest or sense of responsibility for legislating relief. One may try to argue that we had a major social welfare relief program in the latter part of the 19th century when we legislated civil war pension benefits, providing for wounded veterans or their widows, primarily in the North, with support well into the 20th century. But as we have argued in our discussion of American history, this legislation was not targeting poverty, nor did it seek to help all those in need of support, and was very selective. It was a reward for fighting, not a recognition of poverty. The ideological debate over laissez-faire capitalism and the implications of this for allocating funds to alleviate poverty, had a discouraging effect on efforts for reformist legislation. Business leaders were much less willing to support governmental programs to help the poor, in the United States compared to Western Europe. One may try to explain the lack of action by arguing that nation-building in the United States was more important, or that the spirit or "individualism" of American society placed greater responsibility on the individual, and rightly so. But to use these as rationales for the absence of national level concern about and action for the care of the poor, is weak. Our Congress could bring itself to adopt legislation for the Civil War veterans (in the North), but not for the poor. And to claim a greater individualism in America than in the Netherlands, or France, or England does not ring true. The blunt reality is that our national leaders never grew up to accept their responsibility nationally to treat the poor humanely. In Europe they did, even long before the 20th century.

In Chapters 5 and 6 we discuss at length the contrast in the role of the parliamentary and nongovernmental elites in their attitudes toward poverty in the United States compared to those elites in Europe. Free market capitalism resulted in a business elite with little interest in national action. In the United States the labor movement, especially the AFL, showed no interest either. The disinterest by political elites was notorious. In the West European countries political elites became interested in sound welfare and poverty alleviation.

American scholars have documented well this philosophy in the 19th century held by the rich and powerful in the United States. One must remember that in the entire 19th century there was tremendous development and many accomplishments. It was a very busy century. With wars (1812, the Civil War, the Mexican conflict, and in 1898), with the maturing of a new democracy, including the new institutions, new processes, new and liberating political reforms, such as the expansion of the suffrage, the emancipation of the slaves, the development of a civil service, etc. But it was above all a century for the modernization of the economy, laissez-faire capitalism. As our country grew in size and population and embraced the territory to the west, one could argue that our government had no time or sense of urgency about dealing with the problem of the poor. Yet, speaking comparatively, we must emphasize that Western European countries were also in the 19th century undergoing great change—politically, socially, and in the character of their economic system. They were trying to make constitutional monarchies more democratic, the societies were becoming more urban. And they were adjusting to the changes emerging from the industrial revolution. Yet, these European systems were governed by national elites who were much more concerned about the need for social reform and particularly the need to develop ways of relieving the poor. Why the difference?

In a sense, perhaps too simple a sense, what happened in the United States in the 19th century was that big business and wealthy "captains of industry" played a major role in our system. They were interested in unfettered capitalism, unregulated business, operating under the natural laws of supply and demand, of economic self interest, where "competition was the very essence" of the modern society, and the "less government the better." The wealthy business man became the icon of American society. Sidney Fine in his excellent study of the 19th century has a most revealing chapter on "Laissez faire and the American Businessmen." He provides a fascinating study, replete with references and quotations from the businessman of the time, including of course, Carnegie, Rockefeller, Rothchild, and others.[1] He documents carefully their beliefs in these basic principles of capitalism, as well as the consequences for poverty relief which flowed from these economic values. For example, in an appearance before the committee on Education and Labor of the United States Senate in 1885, a prominent business leader stated: "The poor and the weak have to go to the wall to some extent, of course. This is one of the natural laws that we can not get over except by providing for them by charity."[2] As Sidney Fine elaborates the argument, "the doctrine of self interest was particularly attractive to the businessman for it provided him with a truly potent argument to defend the existing order." Andrew Carnegie wrote dramatically how if we left business alone, unregulated, it would lead to the betterment of all. "The millionaires are the bees that make the most honey and contribute most to the hive after they have gorged themselves full."[3] Another business leader added: "The captains of industry are fathers to guide the masses to higher conditions." In fact, of course, they never did much guidance financially! Carnegie was aware of the need for philanthropy, and promised to spend what he had earned each year over $50,000 for the building of university libraries, hospitals and public parks. This was his so-called Gospel of Wealth, but he did not suggest any social welfare reforms. He did feel his gospel might be an answer somewhat to the "unequal distribution of wealth." But there were no proposals from Carnegie and his industrial friends to develop legislation to help all the poor. When asked why did poverty exist in society, their answers were often unbelievably hard. For example, Carnegie argued that the success of a businessman was "a simple matter of honest work, ability, and concentration", which presumably the poor did not have. Worse still was the response of a Standard Oil magnate who said: "Poverty exists because nature or the devil has made some men weak and imbecilic and others lazy and worthless, and neither man nor God can do much for one who will do nothing for himself."[4] These negative views by American businessmen were unfortunately echoed often by Protestant clergy. The renowned minister Henry Ward Beecher is quoted in the New York Times (in 1889) as follows: "God has intended the great to be great and the little to be little. . . . it is a general truth (that) no man in this land suffers from poverty unless it be more than his fault—unless it is his sin."[5] And Bishop Harris of Michigan attacked the idea of state poor relief as "injurious to both the poor and the rich." Relief of this type, he held, encourages "improvidence." No wonder that this convergence of the beliefs of wealthy businessmen and Protestant clergy led the labor leader, Samuel Gompers, to state that laborers were alienated from the church— "They have come to look upon the church and ministry as the apologists and defenders of the wrongs committed against the interests of the people, simply because the perpetrators are the possessors of wealth."[6] With these sentiments and hardened beliefs, and with the dominance of conservative, ungenerous, captains of industry in charge, opposing any state action, is it any wonder that nothing really happened of significance in social reform at the national level in the United States in the 19th century, while much was happening, to the contrary, in Western European systems? As to the distinction between worthy and unworthy poor, it is interesting to note the West European experience. In most countries in the early years there was less inclination to see the poor as paupers and not necessarily deserving of help. But a radical change did occur in some countries. The English as a matter of fact adopted their 1834 Poor Law on that conception of poverty. It was a brutal piece of legislation, denounced by the conservative political leader Disrael as an announcement to the world that "in England poverty is a crime." But England "got over" this conception and by the 20th century took a very humane approach to the poor, seeing them as disadvantaged fellow citizens, victims of the system. This was true of all of these West European nations as their liberal social reform legislative programs reveal. But in a sense the United States elites never quite got over this idea and never completely saw the poor from a humanitarian perspective. Even today we want to get rid of "welfare" while ironically in West Europe they developed laws to provide for welfare! The important observation here is that many of the United States political elites never "got over" this idea that some poor are "unworthy." This is much less true of the American public, as our subsequent analysis will demonstrate. The major question now is how do these differences in historical development play out in the pattern of social reform legislation in these countries, including reforms concerning poverty, as these nations moved in to the latter part of the 19th century, and then into the 20th century? Does history seem to matter?

If one reviews the timing of the adoption of social reform legislation in these countries the picture which emerges is truly remarkable. It is remarkable that so many of the national governments of these European countries were moved to act so early, in contrast to the United States. The accompanying Tables 2.1 and 2.2 display a summary "calendar" of this legislation by country and document what happened. The data reveal how minimal and how late the American effort was. Already by 1900 the West European states had adopted 10 pieces of major legislation, and from 1900 to 1920 they adopted another 15 acts on social reform. Already in 1883 the German Chancellor Otto Von Bismarck pushed through a health insurance law, followed by accident insurance in 1884 and an old age and disability act in 1889. These actions were seen by many as being motivated by Bismarck's concern about rising socialism and public protests. Whether true or not, this legislation was seen as setting the stage for other European states. And indeed in some countries, such as France, there was considerable interest in what Bismarck was doing and some desire to follow suit. Other countries developed their own conceptions of the reform legislation they wanted. And much legislation indeed emerged. The three actions advocated by Bismarck, plus unemployment insurance, were the "Big 4" actions in social reform legislation at that time. However, there was also a beginning of interest in

Table 2.1: The Calendar of Social Reform Legislation (Major Laws) in the U.S. and Western Europe—1870 to 1900

A. National Legislation in the U.S. and Western Europe: 1870 to 1900	
England	Workman's Compensation (1897)
Netherlands	Child Labor (1874)
	Women's Hours (1889)
	Factory Safety (1885)
France	Medical Aid for the Poor (1893)
	Industrial Accident Insurance (1898)
Belgium	Women's and Children's Ind'l Labor Conditions (1889)
Germany	Health Insurance (1883)
	Accident Insurance (1884)
	Old Age Pensions and Disability Insurance (1889)
Sweden	None
United States	None*

*In the United States while there was no national legislation, eight states had "Women's Hours of Work" laws. Note: Not included are new legislation on education, minimum wage laws, housing laws, etc, and amendments to pension laws extending coverage.

other types of legislation. The French adopted an anti-poverty law in 1893, and in 1912 the Dutch legislation provided for medical assistance to the poor. The hours of work for women and children, for example, were regulated. Thus, early versions of some of the "Big 4" social reforms emerged in most of these states by 1920.

In the meantime American congressmen and women as well as United States senators were quiet, not interested in social reform legislation at the national level. The states were one by one adopting laws concerning the working conditions of the women and children, as well as workers compensation for accidents. From 8 to 40 legislatures of American states crafted their own laws in these areas. But these varied greatly in provisions and procedures. No United States national act was adopted until the Social Security Act of 1935. By that time the West European nations had adopted, expanded, amended and thus created legislation which began to deal with the problems of economic inequality and poverty. But there was no action in Washington, D.C. In fact in the period from 1870 to 1920 the scores were 25 national social reform laws for these West European countries and zero (none) for the United States.

As we followed and reported the histories of these countries in their

Table 2.2: The Calendar of Social Reform Legislation (Major Laws) in the U.S. and Western Europe—1900 to 1920

B. National Legislation in the U.S. and Western Europe: 1900 to 1920	
England	Old Age Pension (1908) Health Insurance (1911) Unemployment Insurance (1911)
Netherlands	Industrial Accident (1901) Neglected Children Act (1905) Hours of Work (1910) Medical Aid for Poor (1912)
France	Health Insurance (1902) Old Age Pensions (1910) Public Assistance Law (1905)
Belgium	Accident Insurance (1903) Health Insurance (1912)
Germany	Only Unemployment Insurance in 1927
Sweden	Old Age Pensions (1913) Industrial Accident Insurance (1918)
United States	None*

*In the United States while there was no national legislation, thirty-nine states had "Women's Hours of Work" laws (1900-1909) and forty states had "Workmen's Compensation Laws" and "Mothers' Pension Laws" (1911-20). Note: Not included are new legislation on education, minimum wage laws, housing laws, etc, and amendments to pension laws extending coverage.

struggles to deal with the poverty problems they faced, we noted that toward the close of the 19th century, most Western European countries were still concerned about the adequacy of their approaches. In France they were torn between seeing the poor as criminals or as worthy of help. In the Netherlands the national government was still battling with local government officials and the church over who should deal with the poverty relief needs of their society. In England intellectuals and politicians were despairing of the administration of the 1834 Poor Law and had set up a Royal Commission to study the problem. What seems to have happened in these Western European societies in the latter part of the 19th century is the development of a keen awareness that poverty alleviation was not occurring as well or as adequately as was desired. There was a growing acceptance of the imperative that more needed to be done, and that government should intervene at the national level, that laissez-faire capitalism would never solve, indeed would more likely aggravate, poverty, and that national action was necessary. Aware, thus, of the great need, of the failure, at least in part, of these efforts thus far, and accepting the responsibility of government at the national level to act, they proceeded to design their own strategies for policy action. And almost all of them did act, somewhat experimentally perhaps, but they did adopt their first legislation. This was to be improved and amended later, but they did act—and early. All but Sweden acted before 1900, continuing and adding more benefits for the needy in the 20 year period to 1920.

What is particularly to be noted is that this early legislation was adopted by the 19th century "liberal" and "conservative" politicians, not by the socialists. Indeed, it is true that the socialists were beginning to organize during this period, and some politicians such as Bismarck acted, it is claimed, to keep the socialists at bay. But the elites who cast the votes in the Parliaments of these countries were by and large from the "old school", truly concerned by the problems of the underclass in their societies and determined to provide a proper social provision for them.

The United States Experience to World War I

We may well ask at this point "what was taking place in the United States in the late 19th and early 20th centuries which would explain inaction on poverty at the national (or local) level?" People were certainly aware of the existence of poverty after the Civil War, during Reconstruction, and later. Those returning from the war and widows, despite veterans' benefits in the North, were by no means well off, and the South as we know had extensive poverty. Periodically economic crises increased unemployment and poverty, such as during the Panics of 1873 and of 1893. And scholars as well as political leaders were well aware of it, and writing about it. Henry George's book in 1879, Progress and Poverty sold over 2 million copies, and Edward Bellamy's Looking Backward in 1889 was also widely read. Many problems were facing Americans, yet poverty seemed to evoke less demand for action. Business monopolies were disturbing, the problems of the railroads also demanded attention, as well as agrarian unrest, the need for better education and housing, as well as unemployment and the working conditions in industry.[7] As a result "poverty" seemed to be crowded out of the agenda for public action.

There was also considerable new political organization during this period. The farmers helped create the Granger movement and the Greenback party. Another very prominent third party was the Populists who were especially effective in winning elections in the farm country, getting 8.5% of the national vote for president in 1892. Later, of course, Theodore Roosevelt's Bull Moose party secured 27.5% of the vote in losing the election of 1912. The labor unions were beginning to be more active and their membership was actually increasing. The AFL in 1893 presented a specific set of proposals dealing with political reforms such as the initiative and referendum, the eight hour day, governmental inspection of the mines, employer liability laws, etc. Gompers, head of the AFL, urged the unions to work through government so that by "an intelligent use of the ballot" the workers could "lighten the burden of our economic struggles."[8]

There were also marches on Washington, D.C. One of them organized by Jacob Coxey in 1894, pressed for a solution to unemployment, but it failed miserably, with Coxey sentenced to jail for 20 days and fined five dollars for walking on the grass!

The major leaders, especially in national government, did little to press for the type of social reform which their cousins across the Atlantic were adopting throughout this period. They were more preoccupied with both encouraging and regulating big businesses, which most of them felt was the real goal for development of the country. For example, the government made a gift of 50 million acres to the railroad companies between 1867 and 1877. They accepted generally the central role of businesses and defeated many efforts to reduce big businesses or to restrain capitalism. The presidents and the two major parties accepted with some reservation, laissez-faire capitalism. Theodore Roosevelt was one president who was inclined to propose reforms but never did during his term of office. Only in 1912 when he bolted the Republican Party to run for reelection as a Progressive did he propose reforms. His Progressive Party's convention adopted a platform proposing that "it is time to set the public welfare in the first place." [9] It declared the Progressive Party to be the "instrument of the people, to sweep away old abuses, to build a new and nobler commonwealth." A whole series of proposed changes was then presented, emphasizing heavily new child and female labor laws, improving the conditions of labor, minimum wage and health standards, etc. Unfortunately it was too late for "Teddy" Roosevelt—his New Nationalism lost to the New Freedom of Woodrow Wilson. In the entire period from 1870 to World War I the only relevant action of Congress was in 1892 when it passed a law providing $20,000 for an investigation of housing conditions for the poor in all cities over 200,000 in population.

It seemed that throughout this period, in contrast to what was going on in England and the Continent, in the United States the top elites in government were insensitive to the problems of the poor, unresponsive to the needs of the poor, and engaged in ideological rationalizations to counter any sense of concern about the need for poor relief. This is difficult to comprehend—this extreme gap in humanitarianism between the United States and the countries of Western Europe. We essentially turned our backs on the poor, urging them in this great land of opportunity to find their own way to prosperity. And then came the great Depression. Just before he became president Franklin Delano Roosevelt in a speech in 1932 said" "the country needs and, unless I mistake its temper, demands bold, persistent experimentation." In the years following that speech we finally had a public figure who saw the problem and worked to solve it.

Notes

1. Sidney Fine, *Laissez-Faire and the General-Welfare State: A Study in Conflict in American Thought 1965-1901*, (Ann Arbor, MI: University of Michigan Press), 1957.

2. Fine, *Laissez-Faire and the General-Welfare State*, 101.

3. Fine, *Laissez-Faire and the General-Welfare State*, 102.

4. Fine, *Laissez-Faire and the General-Welfare State*, 98.

5. Fine, *Laissez-Faire and the General-Welfare State*, 119.

6. Fine, *Laissez-Faire and the General-Welfare State*, 124.

7. Many good American historians provide us with the details of this period. Exceptionally useful is Sidney Fine, Laissez Faire and the General Welfare State.

8. Fine, *Laissez-Faire and the General-Welfare State*. 321.

9. Fine, *Laissez-Faire and the General-Welfare State*. 391.

Chapter 3

Attitudes, Beliefs, and Values as an Explanation of the Variance

Scholars have differed over the importance of values (political, economic or social) as explaining governmental policy. Their relevance for the adoption of social reforms might easily be assumed. Skocpol, however, is inclined to dismiss values, arguing they were irrelevant in explaining why England adopted liberal social reforms at the start of the 20th century and the United States did not[1] She claims, with no hard evidence, that both countries were embracing "new liberal" values—yet England acted for reform and the United States did not—therefore, these values, and values generally by implication, had no explanatory power. Yet, no modern social scientist would dismiss values as completely irrelevant. There may be other values (than those Skocpol entertained) which were relevant. And, of course, one would not usually ascribe to values sole responsibility for the adoption of governmental policy. But most certainly values would play some role, as well as a nation's special types of institutions, political processes, and leadership.

There has been considerable controversy over the types of values Americans believe in. McClosky and Zaller argued in 1984 that most Americans are inherently conflicted over their attitudes toward the welfare state because of their commitment to both democracy and capitalism.[2] Others have pointed out the differences between liberals and consecutives in their values on social welfare, conflicted in each case but particularly the liberal democrats, because of their commitment to both humanitarian beliefs and their commitment to individualism.[3]

Culture of course includes many facets of a nation's life and history. One way to describe the normative content or "values" of a culture is to look at the public's beliefs and attitudes. If we do this, and try thereby to identify public attitudes toward poverty and toward the government's role

in relation to poverty, we can see the overtime pattern for the United States
and then compare United States poverty attitudes with those in European
systems. One should note that we are concerned here with the public's
attitudes primarily.

Several scholars have reviewed in detail the data on pubic attitudes.[4]
The earliest usable surveys of public attitudes were made in the 1930s at
the time of the adoption of the United States Social Security Act. Page
and Shapiro provide considerable contributions to this research, Wilens
summarizes his interpretations of these data in the following way:

> Despite their individualistic inclinations, Americans do not oppose
> the welfare state; in fact, they strongly support it. . . . to be sure,
> individualism is alive and well in Americans. . . . but at the same time
> most believe that government can and should play a central role in
> providing both the means for individuals to better themselves, and
> a cushion for times when individuals' own efforts are not enough."[5]

This is quite a creedal statement. It is based on the author's examination of a large number of results from surveys which cover a long period,
from the Thirties to the Nineties. The early public opinion surveys found
strong support in the 1930s for both government social security, and government employment of needy unemployed in the New Deal's special programs
(WPA, CCC, etc.). In 1935 Gallup reported that 89% of the public favored
old age pensions. And this percentage actually increased to 94%. Later
when Gallup modified the question to include both old age pension and
unemployment insurance the percent favorable was still 89%. This level of
support was maintained in a Roper survey in the 1950s. Later, amid all
the pessimistic talk about whether the system would be adequate to the
demands of the "baby boomers" the percentages of support continued to be
high. The public rejected cuts or other changes in social security, continuing
support in the 1980s surveys—at the 80% level. Thus, such data over time
indicate very strong support for these programs of the "welfare state" in
America.[6]

Another type of opinion survey, which comes closer to our concern with
poverty, studied the public's attitude toward helping the unemployed. And
again we find high support in a series of CBS/NYT studies for the statement
that "the government in Washington ought to see to it that everybody who
wants to work can find a job." Yankelovich and others used the wording:
"the passage of a full employment bill in which the government guarantees
a job to everyone who wants to work." In the Seventies all these surveys
reported public support at 70% or higher.[7] Of course, the type of effort
which the public felt the government should make to guarantee and provide jobs required more intensive investigation. Creating public jobs, and
spending more money on job retraining, or giving tax breaks to businesses

which hire unemployed are all proposals which have been endorsed. These studies do demonstrate again that this type of governmental assistance to the needy has become part of the public's willingness to support another aspect of the welfare state.

When we move beyond these findings of public attitudes supporting social security and government assistance to the unemployed, to another welfare state program, namely government responsibility for poor relief, one might be more dubious about public support. Do Americans' liberal social reform values extend to a belief that the government should commit resources to provide assistance beyond employment to the poor? Certain scholars take a negative position on this. Skocpol, for example, states that "American values" extend to government generating jobs and providing job training, but she adds these commitments do not include "providing (poor) relief."[8] If this is so it is a basic contrast to the legislation adopted in England and West European countries, which assert a blanket governmental commitment to take care of all the poor citizens in their country.

What do American surveys of public attitudes reveal on this question? The evidence seems to rebut scholars like Skocpol. In the 1930s and 1940s Roper found high support for the belief that the government should "provide for all people who have no other means of obtaining a living" (65% to 81% support).[9] From this early evidence, support continued even stronger in later years. In 1976-77 Harris's survey found very high agreement that "(it's) not right to let people who need welfare go hungry" (96% agree). Surveys in the Eighties and Nineties reported that there was positive support for the proposition that "there must be substantial government involvement to handle the problem of poverty" (85%) and "the government has a responsibility to take care of the poor" (71% agree). And in 1996 a New York Times Poll used the following statement in probing this matter: "It is the responsibility of the government to take care of people who can't take care of themselves" (66% support). Further, it is interesting that when it is proposed that the problems of the poor can be taken care of by "volunteer efforts" only 15% agree. There is some variation over time in these figures, but it seems clear, as Page and Shapiro conclude, "most Americans do support monetary assistance directly to poor people." It is true that most Americans detest "welfare" and refuse generally to support government funding for "welfare." The welfare bum is a stereotype in Americans' minds—people on welfare, they say, are lazy, won't work, cheat the system, and do not deserve support. But when the question is phrased in terms of "poor" people, and "poor" relief, the support is very positive. And has been so for 60 to 70 years.

These findings do indeed reveal a high level of support for government expenditures "to care for the poor, to feed the hungry, to take care of people who can't take care of themselves," etc. These statements are often very general, and few specifics as to what such poor relief entails and how far the government's responsibility goes. In West European systems the legislation commits the government to provide to all citizens, as a matter of right, a decent standard of living, or "social minimum." While the conditions under which such "open-ended" poor relief is provided are not spelled out carefully, nevertheless, this is blanket commitment and responsibility which these European governments have adopted. (See for example the 1965 Dutch law, the 1948 British law, the 1988 French law, etc.).

It is interesting to look at variations within the publics in the United States and the Western European countries. If we disaggregate these publics by income levels, we will see quite a difference for the United States and Western Europe for example. That there is a gulf or divide within the United States public is clear, and more pronounced than in Europe. If we look at the level of support for each of these statements by those with low and high incomes, we see quite a different picture (Table 3.1). Indeed it appears that the American public has a "bifurcated" attitude and value structure on this question of government aid for the needy.[10]

Table 3.1: Support for Anti-Poverty Governmental Action in Four Nations, By Low and High Income (1987)

Average level of support for Government Action to Provide Poor Relief (%)	US	UK	Ger.	Neth.	US compared to European mean
Low Income	56	72	78	72	-19
High Income	27	50	69	58	-32
Difference	29	22	9	14	

Source: Keene and Ladd, 1990.

Several critical findings emerge from these data.

1. The income level is a critical variable, in the United States particularly, in explaining system differences in attitudes to poor relief.

2. The difference in anti-poverty attitudes varies by income level in all countries, but the differential is largest in the United States.

3. Actually in these European countries 50% or more of those with high incomes support "liberal" governmental action on poverty, which in the United States it is only 27%.

4. While the public in the United States has not been as completely "socialized" as are the Europeans to government action, a majority are clearly in support of such action.

Key questions, then, which emerge from this are: Why is it that the more affluent in West European countries have more liberal values than the affluent in the United States? And is this a possible explanation for the failure of anti-poverty legislation in the United States, and support for such legislation in Europe? There does certainly seem to be a divide between income groups, a class-based bias. When the difficult, specific, "tough" questions are asked in the United States on whether the government should assume specific responsibility for the poor, in the United States the large majority of the public (with low or moderate incomes) are definitely in favor, but the wealthy in the United States oppose such governmental generosities. In Europe, both the poor and the affluent are more likely to say "yes", giving the humanitarian response.

One final basic point should be added to this analysis: the poor in the United States are less likely to vote or engage in political activity than is the case in Europe. Thus, the poor in the United States have less political influence, are less likely to be seen as constituents whom our representatives in Washington have to be responsive to, and are not well organized to try to assert their influence. Thus, the poor are less likely in the United States to be "taken into consideration" by policy makers than is the case in Europe. Further, voting turnout is much higher in all these European nations than in the United States. Recently, except for the 2004 election, we can scarcely get 50% of the eligible voters to go to the polls in national elections; in Britain, the Netherlands, Sweden, Germany, France and Belgium the turnout is usually 70% or better (reaching over 80% in some elections).

Particular analyses over the years of the link of income level to voting, reveal the lower rate of the poor again and again. In 1948 (Presidential election) when election surveys just began, V.O. Key found that while 47% of the lower income levels reported a vote, for the well-to-do the figure was 80%.[11] The identical percentage was reported in surveys in the Seventies (46%–86%). Sidney Verba and his colleagues at Harvard published an excellent study, Participation and Political Equality in 1995 which explained the extent of political activity of the poor compared to the affluent in American society. The findings are presented below.[12]

% Engaging in Activities	Low Income Respondents	High Income Respondents
Campaign work	4	17
Campaign contributions	6	56
Contacted officials	25	50
Community contacts (informal)	13	38
Affiliated with a political organization	29	73

In a very recent study, Verba has presented new data on this point. The differentials in political activity and potential influence by income level, were as follows:[13]

Table 3.2: Variation in Public Opinion by Income Level in the United States

% Emerging in Political Activity	The Very Poor (received means-tested benefits)	Those with no financial needs
Voters	6	43
Contacts	6	40
Contributed money to parties or candidates	1	56

Type of activity or attitude (%)	Income Level under £1,000	£10,000 to £30,000	Over £30,000
1. Was an active party member	24	24	25
2. Favored more government expenditures "to get rid of poverty"	80	79	82

Verba observes from these data that "for those who received means-tested benefits and for those in poverty, there is fairly severe underrepresentation." In European countries, although comparable studies are difficult to find, it is fairly clear from available studies that there are not such large voting participation differences by income as in the United States. And as we stated before the support for government policy to aid the poor has in the past, and continues today, to be at similarly high levels irrespective of income level. In a fairly recent study in England, the authors found precisely these two results again:[14] And this was a study of the Conservative Party! The contrast with the well-to-do public in the United States is striking!

We conclude this section with the observation that there is considerable evidence that over time the American public has expressed often in response to survey questions that it supports government assistance to the poor, in a variety of ways. There is a consistent value orientation which one might call a humanitarian value orientation of concern for the poor. It is not as strong as for Western European publics, but it is clearly a major value. Our research has revealed that in the United States the affluent public is much less concerned than the middle and lower income strata. And this is contrary to what we find in Europe, where the wealthy strongly support poor relief. We discovered also in the scholarly research on this subject that in the United States the poor stand in contrast to the rich also in their level of voting and political activity, and this is also in contrast to the findings in European research. Thus one cannot generalize by saying that "the American public would never support legislation to take care of the poor." This is not factually correct. One can well say that it is much harder in the United States to mobilize support for comprehensive poverty legislation than in Western Europe. But it can be done. In fact it was done when under Lyndon Johnson's "War on Poverty" in the Sixties we passed: AFDC act, food stamps, Medicaid and Medicare. Why have we not done anything as significant in the United States Congress as this since the 1960s? What stands in the way?[15]

Notes

1. Skocpol, *Social Policy in the United States: Future Possibilities in Historical Perspective* (Princeton, NJ: Princeton University Press, 1995) 80-81.

2. Herbert McCloskey and John Zaller, *The American Ethos: Public Attitudes Toward Capitalism and Democracy* (Cambridge, MA.: Harvard, 1984).

3. Adam Berinsky, "Silent Voices: Social Welfare Policy Opinions and Political Equality in America." *American Journal of Political Science.* 46, no. 2, (April 2002), 276-287.

4. See particularly Benjamin Page and Robert Shapiro, *The Rational Public: Fifty Years of Trends in Americans' Policy Preferences* (Chicago, IL.: University of Chicago Press, 1992), 117-171; Martin Gilens, *Why Americans Hate Welfare; Race, Media, and Politics of Anti Poverty Policy*, (Chicago, IL. University of Chicago Press, 1999). 1–2.

5. Gilens, *Why Americans Hate Welfare*, 1-2.

6. See Page and Shapiro *The Rational Public*, for most of these survey results, 118-119.

7. Page and Shapiro *The Rational Public*, 122-123.

8. Skocpol, *Social Policy in the United States*, 237.

9. For these data see Page and Shapiro, *The Rational Public*, 124-125, also Gilens, *Why Americans Hate Welfare*, 38.

10. Karilyn Keene and Everett C. Ladd, eds., "The Public Opinion Report", *American Enterprise*, April, 1990. These are 1987 data.

11. Key, Vladimir O. Jr., *Politics, Parties and Pressure Groups*, (New York: Crowell), 1952, 572.

12. Sidney Verba, Kay Lehman Schlozman and Henry E. Brady *Voice and Equality: Civic Volunteerism in American Politics*, (Cambridge, MA: Harvard University Press. 1995.) 190.

13. Sidney Verba, *Participation and Participatory Equality: Why Do We Want it? Why Might We Not?* (Paper presented at the University of Michigan, 10 April, 2003), 21-22, Table 3.

14. Paul Whitely, Patrick Seyd and Jeremy Richardson, *True Blues: The Politics of Conservative Party Membership*, (Oxford: Clarendon Press, 1994), 106-143.

15. The nature of the values and attitudes of political elites is discussed in Chapters 4 and 5. The polarization of the leaders (in partisan terms) is demonstrated, as well as the differences between American and European elites.

Chapter 4

Political Institutions As Explanations For the Contrast in Anti-Poverty Legislation in Western Europe and the United States

So far in our analysis we have arrived at two major observations which may help us explain the variances in the commitment to poverty relief in our seven countries. Our historical analysis suggests that, from the dim past to the 20th century, in West Europe both masses and elites were gradually, although not continuously, socialized to the need to care for the poor and for national level governments to accept responsibility for poor relief than in the United States. Our second suggestive finding is that the pattern of liberal social reform values, held by the public, was probably delayed in the United States, emerging much later than in Western Europe. Yet, our examination of the data from surveys of the attitudes of the publics in the United States and West Europe reveal that (from the 1930's on when such surveys were reliable) American citizens manifested considerable support for government action to help the poor, indicating majority acceptance of such humanitarian aid. But, there is one possibly important difference–in the United States the poorer class has a significantly lower level of political participation in politics, including voting, than in Western Europe. And this may be linked to less responsiveness by political leaders in the United State to advocate more complete relief for the poor.

Obviously, these two explanations are not enough. How did these two differentials find manifestation in governmental action–with European countries accepting virtual blanket commitments to care for the poor, while the United States government has not been willing to accept this responsibility, in fact has rejected it? And thus has not by its policies brought the poverty

37

rate down to the level it is in Western Europe.

Some scholars feel that "institutional contexts" are important to study. Skocpol: "the structural features of the United States have. . . . powerfully set overall institutional limits for social provision in the United States." Yet, she adds this is only the starting point and one must also study "political struggles." If we do this we can discover, she says, how "the American distinctive state structure has influenced possibilities for collective action. . . ."[1] While this statement of her approach is general and inclusive enough to be acceptable to many, one wonders whether it would not make more sense to state flatly that the "American system" in all its special characteristics (political, economic, sociological) is what we should study, and what we should contrast to Western Europe, if we are to find a "system explanation" to variations in social welfare policy. Yet, the major question is—how much of American social reform behavior can we blame on the workings of the political system?

It is important to remember that these systems are similar in basic respects. They are democracies, all emerging from monarchic traditions to the establishment of popular-based governments, based on the rule of law, belief in liberty, equality, social justice, freedom of opportunity for all, etc. All of them created representative systems of government with elected leaders responsible for governmental action and responsible to, as well as representative of, the masses. Governments presumably rest on "the consent of the governed." In addition, all these systems embraced free market capitalism, although the movement to industrial capitalism was delayed more in some systems than in others. The particular directions which capitalism took had already varied somewhat as these systems developed their economic systems in the 20th century. All of these free societies already in the latter part of the 19th century began to be confronted with the same basic question. In a free, democratic society, with their publics becoming more and more active and assertive, and as the free capitalists prospered greatly, amassing huge incomes from profits,—how was the "economic surplus" to be shared? Should capitalists contribute some or much of the "economic surplus" to the improvement of the welfare of those members of society who could not participate in, or benefit from, the successes of the capitalist state? Should capitalists become "welfare capitalists" or not? That for us is a crucial dilemma to consider here.

In certain special ways the American system was distinctive. For instance, we never had a viable Socialist Party with any real electoral appeal. Its highest percent of the vote was in 1912 when it received 6% of the vote for President. One might well argue that this was a critical difference, because in Europe either Social Democratic or Labor parties had many more members and votes. Yet, one should be reserved about using this as a critical difference. For one reason, because some of the social reforms in Europe were achieved before the socialists were major parties. In the pre 1900 period Bismarck's social reforms were not achieved through socialist party actions (although it is alleged that Bismarck was worried about the emerging socialists and he feared that they might organize protests against his regime). Similarly the Dutch Poor Law of 1912 is not attributable to the socialists, nor the early legislation in England. In fact, it was not until the 1930's in Sweden, and after World War II in the other countries that the Socialists gathered strength and played a greater role. Even then, however, the Socialists were not alone in pushing through social reforms. In the Netherlands after the war they had four cabinets led by Willem Drees, the Labor leader, but these, one must remember, were coalition cabinets, with three religious parties working with the Labor Party. Drees's Labor Party's strength in the Dutch Parliament was 25% to 28% from 1945 to 1952, so he had to rely on these leaders from the more conservative parties to get his social reform legislation adopted. Only in the case of Sweden was the Social Democratic party quite dominant, heading the cabinets from 1932 to 1976, but even it had to form a "bloc" because rarely did it have 50% of the vote. This underscores one major point to remember. The Socialists were very instrumental in some countries, but rarely could they muster enough strength to "go it alone." The social reform values were held by the leaders of many non socialist parties also, and this was crucial for the success of social reforms. Even in England under Margaret Thatcher the Conservatives did not really attempt to radically reverse their system. In the Netherlands it is interesting to note that when the government passed the 1963 law of "complete governmental responsibility" for the poor, there were no labor members in the government.

One should note above all that in the United States with no viable Socialist party, we adopted a great deal of "socialist" legislation—from WPA in 1933 to Social Security and unemployment insurance in 1935, to Medicaid in 1965, and food stamps in 1965, and the SSI (Supplemental Security Insurance) in 1972, etc. True we do not have national health insurance nor real satisfactory relief for all the poor. But one cannot say that the absence of a Socialist Party was a basic deciding factor in this. Other factors seemed to obstruct complete social reform legislation in the United States.

Another factor cited by some scholars as an explanation of differences in social reform actions by countries is the strength of labor organizations, and the extent to which this organization was nationally centralized.[2] There is no doubt that differences exist. If one looks at the membership of unions (as a percent of the labor force) Sweden's union membership grew from 1930 to 1970 from 20% to 75%. Belgium's union membership grew to 51% by 1975 and the United Kingdom to 44% during the same period. But the

United States grew only from seven percent in 1930 to 23% in 1970. Yet it is difficult to argue that the strength and aggressive role of labor unions were key distinctive factors in explaining why the United States did not adopt as comprehensive social welfare legislation as West European countries did. The level of union membership in France in 1970 was only 15% and in Germany 34%, as it was also in the Netherlands. Also, in the Netherlands there were for a long time separate Catholic, Protestant, and Socialist unions. Yet, despite these differences European systems did get legislation passed which included significant poor relief programs. On the other hand, we in the United States did manage to pass key reforms (such as the Social Security Act of 1935) despite weak labor unions. It is difficult to generalize therefore that the extensiveness of labor union organization, while no doubt helpful at certain times, was the key difference between countries adopting poor relief and the United States. This does not seem to have been the critical requisite. A third type of argument, involving "system" differences which contrast the United States and West European systems emphasizes the institutions and process which "separate" or "divide" the location and exercise of power in the United States much more than in these other countries. The United States is described as a pluralized system where power is shared between the federal government in Washington with the 50 states, where the President and the Congress may represent different parties and ideologies (leading to presidential vetoes and Congressional refusals to act). The Presidency in the United States is often referred to as a powerful force for inaction and a source of such conflict with Congress that action is difficult. Having a nationally elected President (every 4 years) with a national constituency, and 435 Congressional representatives elected by 435 constituencies (every 2 years), and a Senate of 100 members elected by 50 states (every 6 years), makes it difficult to coordinate efforts and achieve unified and consistent action on legislation. In addition there is a Supreme Court with power to declare Presidential and Congressional actions unconstitutional. These structural features, it is argued, make new and positive and consistent social reform legislation difficult to accomplish.

If examined carefully, this argument is really not tenable, since it must again be evaluated in terms of how our system has actually functioned. The American "federal" system has never inhibited the national government from acting on welfare legislation. The state may be asked to administer a national law and may do this in a way which is less effective and fair than it should be. But that does not mean that the national government has assigned away its power to act. When the states are asked by the federal government to share the costs of poor relief (as in the food stamp program) problems may develop, but the national government has the power to deal with such a problem.

The American system of "separation of powers" between the President, Congress, the Senate, and the Supreme Court, is claimed to be "exceptional", and indeed in many respects it is. But whether it is the major obstacle to the adoption of satisfactory anti-poverty legislation (or national health insurance) is highly questionable. It may be a system which makes such action difficult, and requires therefore a different strategy for success in getting legislation passed. But it does not, and certainly has not, prevented legislative accomplishment. In an interesting 1991 study Mayhew presents strong evidence that despite "divided government" the United States is able to pass much of its most significant legislation. He studied over 200 legislative cases from 1946 to 1990 and found that of the legislation which was introduced in a context of "divided government" (President for one party and one or both houses of Congress for the other party) 84% of the proposed legislation passed (in contrast, surprisingly, to only 68% for legislation introduced in a context of "unified government").[3] It is notable that among those laws passed were disability insurance (1956), Food Stamps (1970), Supplemental Social insurance (1972), as well as many other very important pieces of legislation, such as Civil Rights in 1965. Mayhew concluded that it makes "very little difference what the party control pattern in Congress was" for most of this very important legislation. Thus, to argue that the so-called unique American structure or system of political power by itself explains our failure to pass certain types of social reform legislation, is just not credible.

This brings us to the next argument, to a feature of the American system; our two party system which combined with our type of election system (a single member district, non-PR system) is alleged to make social reform legislation difficult. All seven countries in this study are different in the types of party and election systems which they have. Most have multi-party systems and proportional representation election systems. The British system is perhaps closest to ours. It is often called a "two-party" system despite the fact that ten or more parties have won seats in the House of Commons in recent elections. The English have the same SMD election system that we have. But the English party system is different in certain critical respects. Ours is a "duopoly", that is only the Republicans or Democrats win seats to the Congress or Senate (although there is an occasional "independent"). In the English system the winning party usually has a majority of seats, despite many opposition parties. Further, the structure of the English party system is different—one of its two major parties is historically quite "left of center"—such as the Labor party, so the ideological conflict and debate in the British system has a special character. Finally, the British parties operate in a parliamentary system, in which the dominant party in the House of Commons is truly in control of the government, in contrast to our presidential and "checks and balances" system.

It is often argued that under the American system it is very difficult for a minority group or interest, particularly if it is lower class, to get a voice, a hearing, and strong representation of its policy proposals. Each of the two parties, the Democrats and Republicans, is a pluralistic coalition of special interests, with some group interests overlapping both parties, other groups distinctively located in one party and more likely to get a "hearing" and policy action in either the Democratic or Republican parties. For a minority group interest to be successful it needs to be well organized, well led, perceived as having some "voting clout", and, ideally, member representation in Congress. Alternatively, if possible, it may join other groups in a subcoalition within the party. The probability of a successful bipartisan strategy is low.[4]

It can well be claimed that the American type of two-party system functions in such a way as to not facilitate, but rather provide obstacles to, achieving the type of policy action on poor relief advocated here. First, the voting power of the relevant interest group is very limited, then the interest is usually poorly organized and, third, its sympathetic representation in Congress may be minimal. (These aspects of our system will be discussed and elaborated on in the next sections of our analysis.)

Is the two-party system in the United States, therefore, the real obstacle? No doubt it is a complicated institutional gauntlet through which to maneuver easily. But, per se one cannot say that this institutional arrangement and the processes associated with it constitute the real reason why we have not adopted a comprehensive anti-poverty program. As Schattschneider, a famous American theorist of parties, said, our pluralist system functions with an "upper class" tendency, and the people with the greatest social needs are less likely to be taken into consideration by the organized groups and actors playing a major role in our party politics.[5] Despite this liability, however, we should not forget the great achievements and great legislation passed by our Congress under this type of two-party system. From 1789 to today our national party system has originated and adopted great laws, including, those which constitute a part of our social welfare system—from the Social Security Act of 1935 under Franklin D. Roosevelt and Medicaid and Medicare under Lyndon Johnson, as well as other legislative actions extending and improving such laws. In 1935 the Social Security Act was passed by close to 90% of Republicans and Democratic members of Congress.

Our basic point here, as we conclude this section, is that one must search elsewhere than our political institutions for satisfactory answers to our question. Our historical analysis has suggested how and why we were so slow in adopting a social welfare program. Our analyses of public opinion has documented the level of public support for aid for the poor. These are only partial paths to the truth. And the same may be said for the role of the American two-party system—it is by no means the real answer. Therefore, we present now, our exploration of a different theory, a different answer to our problem in recent years, our failure to commit to a comprehensive anti-poverty program. We want to focus on the political and economic elite system in America, a system which in our opinion, instead of confronting the poverty problem frontally, has instead avoided a complete solution to it assiduously. As a consequence we still have 37 million Americans living in poverty. This is 12.7% of the population, the same percentage as 30 years ago. In a sense the title of Schattschneider's book, *The Semisovereign People* points to the real problem—the inadequacies of our system of political representation in the United States.

Notes

1. Theda Skocpol, *Social Policy in the United States: Future Possibilities in Historical Perspective*, (Princeton, NJ: Princeton University Press, 1995), 25, 84-85.

2. John D. Stephens, *The Transition From Capitalism to Socialism*, (Urbana, IL: University of Illinois Press, 1986), 89-128.

3. David Mayhew, *Divided We Govern: Party Control, Lawmaking, and Investigations, 1946-1990* (New Haven, CN: Yale University Press, 1991), 122.

4. For further elaboration of this theory see Samuel J. Eldersveld and Hanes Walton Jr., *Political Parties in American Society* (Boston: Bedford/St. Martin's, 2000), 178.

5. Elmer Schattschneider, *The Semisovereign People: A Realist's View of Democracy in America* (New York: Holt, Rinehart, and Winston, 1960), 31-34, 105.

Chapter 5

The Role of Political Elites and the Elite System in Explaining Poverty Relief in the United States and Western Europe

While history can have a causal relevance, as well as public values, in our opinion it is elites who in the last analysis are responsible. In the United States political leadership sometimes functions differently than in Europe. If poor relief is not provided for properly or adequately in the United States the political elites must carry the burden of guilt. Our point, we repeat, is that our leaders are at fault, not the system (although the system may condition elite performance). It is our national leaders (the President and Congress) who took no action on poverty in the latter part of the 19th century, while national leaders in most Western European countries did act. It is our national leaders (President and Congress) who did nothing to relieve poverty from 1900 to 1930, while European leaders did. Not until the great Depression thrust the problem of poverty on our national leaders, after 1929, did they act. Then World War II arrived and we did not again successfully address the problem until the 1960s. It was our national leadership which failed us. Elite behavior (perceptions, values, sense of responsibility, intellectuality, motivation, and drive to act) has been the paramount cause for the incompleteness of our anti-poverty programs today.

It is necessary to keep in mind the character, composition, and political context of our national political elite, in contrast to Western Europe, in order to understand in part at least why our political elite in Washington fails to act effectively on poverty. The focus here is on the legislative and executive as individuals, rather than the nature of the institutions (the Congress and the Presidency) which we have described in the previous chapter. Our characterization here of our political leader is derived from the many studies which have been done by American scholars over the years, and familiar to those who have analyzed congressional and presidential leaders in the United States.

First, one must recognize the social class bias in the recruitment and selection of members of Congress and presidents, historically and still today. For example studies have shown that in the early days down to the 1950s United States presidential cabinets had an upper class bias. Whereas only 3% of cabinet members in the United States came from working class backgrounds, the percentages for Britain was 21% and for Germany 11%. For United States Senators in 1940 only 4% came from labor, while 27% had a business background and this was true all the way back to 1900 when 34% were "business."[1] In a study we completed in the 1970s of the parliaments and bureaucratic elites in Europe and the United States we found that left-of-center and center parties in Europe recruited far more legislators with lower and working class backgrounds than did the United States. The data on social origins are as follows:[2]

Members of Parliament or Congress From Lower/Middle Class					
Country (Party)	US (Dems)	UK (Labor)	France (PCP)	Ger. (SPD)	Neth. (Labor)
% from a lower/work-ing class back-ground	14	46	20	52	55

In addition, 32% of European MPs had no university education, while this was true of only 9% in the United States. This contrast is striking! Aspirants to national office from lower class backgrounds obviously are much more successful and actively recruited in West Europe than in the United States.

Second, it is important to keep in mind how expensive it is to run for national office in the United States. campaign finance legislation has been evaded by the contribution of large sums which are not regulated. There is current litigation before the court again over a new law adopted by Congress in 2002, but this has by no means reduced the costs of running for office. The cost of running for national office has increased greatly over the years, as these data reveal.[3]

Average Contributions to Candidates For Each Seat (in $000)		
Year	House of Representatives	United States Senate
1972	51.7	353.9
1980	148.3	1,079.3
1992	358.9	2,166.0
1996	511.0	3,274.9
2000	533.0	4,560.0

In the campaign for the presidency in 2000, the pre-nomination campaigns (primaries mostly) cost a total of 326 million dollars for all fifteen candidates (Gore 42.5 million dollars and Bush 89.1 million dollars.) In the actual campaigns after the national conventions, Gore and Bush spent 166.7 million dollars. The national committees of the parties in 2000 reported they spent an additional 780 million dollars "hard" and "soft" money. If one adds to these presidential campaign expenses and national committee finance activities the 384.6 million dollars for House campaigns and the 298.6 million dollars for Unites States Senate campaigns, the total rises to an incredible two billion dollars spent on the activity of parties and candidates at the national level. And this includes only those expenditures fully disclosed! How then can eligible and able persons contest for national office if they cannot access these types of resources? Only if they are recruited and sponsored by affluent friends, or business corporations, or unions, or if they are recruited by the parties themselves, who will cover their campaign costs.

In contrast to this American system, in European countries campaigns cost much less. Indeed, there are limits specified for the amounts that are permitted to be spent by a candidate. In the Netherlands, for example, limits on broadcasting, and no interest by corporations in influencing elections result in much smaller expenditures. Some years ago it was estimated that a national election could cost about 6 to 8 million guilders. Andeweg and Irwin report that there is "social pressure against business contributions." The parties therefore rely heavily on membership dues to support their activities. In other countries, such as Germany, more is spent on campaigns, but nothing of the magnitude of US expenditures.

In an earlier comparative study of party finance by Alexander he presented these data for some of our countries—expenditures by the major parties in elections in the 1980s:

- Netherlands–21 million guilders for the three main parties

- Britain–5 million pounds for the two major parties

In the same years in the 1980s our parties spent $275 million on presidential elections (1984) and $400 million on congressional elections (1986).[4] In

Western Europe, thus, the recruitment of "lower class" candidates is not limited by affluence. Plus the parties take a liberal and inclusive stand in selecting candidates for office, particularly conscious of the need for persons who are for the working class, because they desire a representative group of candidates from their party in Parliament.[5]

A third set of data on the occupational composition of Congress is important in this regard. Studies have shown the presence of relatively wealthy upper middle class of both houses of Congress. A recent study, for instance, reported that in the Nineties 37% of the House members were in business or banking, and 42% had law careers. There were similar percentages for the Senate.[6] We will return to this in our discussion of the business elite in the next chapter. It should be added here that the occupational composition of European Parliaments is quite different—many fewer from business.

One might well conclude from the three sets of data just presented that the probability of finding many "liberals" in the United States Congress interested in social welfare and, particularly, in anti-poverty legislation, is low. But political science research has indicated that social status does not primarily determine whether a legislator is "liberal" or "conservative." Those coming from middle class and upper middle class backgrounds can subsequently be much less conservative than expected, in fact can take liberal policy positions. To what extent does that seem to be true? We actually have many "liberals" in Congress, as the voting records of most Democrats and some Republicans reveal. But today, and often in the past, ours is a polarized Congress ideologically. And the same is true of national party organization leaders. Recent studies of such leaders reveal this sharp division of opinion. The accompanying data (Table 5.1) reveals this "divide" is very highly significant.[7] The table reports the results of interviews with these leaders, as well as with a sample of party identifiers in the public.

If one looks at these data carefully, it may be possible to get answers to our key questions. These are data from 1992, when Clinton won the presidency and the Democrats won a majority in the House and Senate. Extrapolating from these data one can conclude that there was indeed a large percentage of liberals among the Democrats on both of these questions, although some were marginal liberals (near the midpoint of the scale). More liberals on the health care issue, interestingly, than on social welfare. Perhaps 60% of the Democrats were solid "liberals." But the Republicans are conservative on both issues, and one cannot create a majority in this Congress, from these data, in favor of these two key social welfare issues. And what is troubling is that the followers are less liberal (74 to 50 and 82 to 65) in the Democratic Party. Which implies less "pressure from below" for policy change than one would hope.

Thus, on this suggestive evidence we clearly have a very conflicted na-

Table 5.1: Social Welfare Attitudes of National Party Representatives and Followers in 1992 (in %)

A. *Support for Social Welfare Services (scale 1 to 7)*

Party:	Democrat %		Republican %	
Scale	Delegates	Followers	Delegates	Followers
1–*More services*	30.4	13.2	0.5	4.5
2	26.6	13.6	0.5	5.1
3	17.0	23.0	4.0	11.7
4	11.8	33.7	13.7	25.7
5	8.1	9.3	22.3	25.0
6	3.2	4.2	26.4	18.2
7–*Fewer services*	2.8	3.1	32.1	9.9
Mean Scale	2.6	3.4	5.6	4.6

B. *Support for National Health Insurance (scale 1 to 7)*

Party:	Democrat %		Republican %	
Scale	Delegates	Followers	Delegates	Followers
1–*Government insurance*	44.3	31.3	2.2	13.6
2	22.2	19.0	2.8	8.1
3	15.4	24.3	5.0	12.2
4	9.1	8.1	12.5	20.3
5	4.4	7.1	9.7	17.3
6	2.5	5.0	19.5	14.0
7–*Private insurance*	2.1	5.3	48.2	14.4
Mean Scale	2.2	2.8	5.8	4.2

tional leadership ideologically, particularly with reference to these key policy areas. The only mildly surprising finding is that the Republican followers are more liberal than their leaders. Indeed, a third of them favor health insurance and a fifth seems to be willing to have more social welfare services. The only other positive note is that if we compare the 1992 findings with 1984, when the identical study was done we find that there is progress. Whereas in 1984 the Democratic leaders were only 59% liberal on national health insurance, in 1992 82% favored it. But the Republican leaders have not changed much; they were even more conservative on social welfare in 1992 than in 1984.

In reflecting on these data one can start to wonder what happened in 1993 when the Democrats won the presidency and Congress. What happened to the large number of "liberal" Democratic legislators (74% on social welfare issues)? One never heard from them! Why not? Not sincere? Or unwilling to battle? Too pressured by certain forces not to take action? Poorly led? In 1994 the Republicans came back to control of Congress and our Democrats, including President Clinton, finally settled for the 1996 law (the one which was to "change welfare as we know it"). By 2002 the Census Bureau tells us poverty is increasing!

There is no question but that the ideological polarization at the national level is a major obstacle to poverty reduction. One doesn't find this often in Europe. In Britain, as Bochel points out, under the Conservative government of Margaret Thatcher "there were real increases in government spending on the National Health Service and personal social services" (from 1979 to 1984). A 1987 survey of MP's revealed that while Conservatives took a more narrow view of "the ideal role of the state in welfare provision" 70% of the Conservatives approved the "safety net" provision "to meet genuine need only," while almost 100% of the Labor MP's supported poor relief, 56% at a higher national minimum of benefits. There was very little dissent, but rather majority support for the anti poverty program (although somewhat more limited by the Conservatives).[8]

In the Netherlands, there was also strong support for a policy of higher taxes in order to provide better services for the poor. In a 1972 study of "Issue consensus" among the parties, Dutch scholars found 68% support for all MP's combined, ranging from 97% for the Labor party to 62% for two confessional parties, with 85% for the "center" Catholic Party. One small party on the right (the VVD) opted primarily for lower taxes (69%) and only six percent for higher taxes to provide social welfare services.[9] This absence of fundamental dissensus in these European systems on the provision for social welfare services, stands in contrast to the United States. Why should this be so? Why so much more consensus on social welfare reform in Europe than in the United States? This is a question we will return to later in this discourse.

Historically, the problem of getting social welfare legislation through the United States Congress is partially because of ideological differences within the two parties, as well as regional differences. The "Southern Democratic" faction within the Democratic Party was in the past, particularly, a critical problem. A brief case history of the adoption of the Social Security Act of 1935 will illustrate the differentials. Roosevelt took up this cause in 1934, stating blatantly "there is no reason why everybody in the United States should not be covered. I see no reason why every child, from the day he is born, shouldn't be a member of the social security system." Working with Frances Perkins, his secretary of Labor, he set the wheels in motion. By the following January they put the plan before Congress. But the proposed legislation had to be cut back because Secretary Perkins said people were not ready yet for "the universal approach." It was an Act providing only partial coverage (not until the 1960s did coverage become broader). Compulsory health insurance was not proposed because it was feared that would be difficult to adopt at this time. Conservatives in Congress immediately sought to kill the proposed Social Security bill—as "a violation of traditional American values of thrift, initiative, and self-help." [10] It was suggested that all Americans would have to wear a dog tag with a social security number on it. It was a law which would rob "a thrifty Peter to pay an improvident Paul." After much criticism the Act was passed on August 14.

We must remember this dramatic vote in Congress on the Social Security Act. It was supported in the House by 96% of the Democrats and 81% of the Republicans; in the Senate by 74% of the Republicans and all but one Democrat! What a victory for humanity! Never again would a social welfare bill pass Congress with such overwhelming bi-partisan support.

After that vote there came the hard part—getting a new tax bill passed which would "reach directly into the pockets of the wealthy and the corporations"—an inheritance tax, a gift tax, increased individual taxes, and corporate levies linked to the size of the corporation. The tax on business Roosevelt felt was necessary because the New Deal had been approved by the business interests. This resulted in a "whirlwind of protest." William Randolph Hearst blasted FDR and ordered his editors to call this the "Raw Deal"; the bill was labeled socialistic. J.P. Morgan's family rejected newspapers with pictures of FDR shown. The opposition forced the reduction of corporation tax rates and the elimination of the inheritance tax. But FDR made it clear that he would "use taxation as a weapon of social change."

Another case during Kennedy's administration illustrates how a major social reform law was scuttled. In 1962 Kennedy decided to press for a Medicare bill. It was opposed by a coalition of Republicans and Southern Democrats. The latter had control of the Rules Committee in the House, which refused to report the proposed bill out for floor action. Democratic speaker Sam Rayburn was having difficulty forcing the Rules Committee to approve the bill for debate in the House. Only by enlarging the committee and making new, favorable, appointments could he overrule the Rules Committee Chair. The Republican Party in the House (under Charles Halleck) came out against the bill. The Chamber of Commerce came out against it, as did the National Association of Manufacturers, and the American Medical Association. "The infighting became vicious." [11] The President made several calls to rally support. It carried in the House 217-212, even though 64 Democrats voted against the President. But the Senate had the final word. The AMA attack on the President and his bill was bitter. The President responded and talked to individual "swing" Senators. But it was not enough and the Senate voted 52-48 against. The humane instincts of 1935 did not return to Congress! Kennedy considered the loss of his Medicare bill one of his most discouraging defeats. We had to wait for Lyndon Johnson's administration for Medicare to be adopted.

These examples of the conditions for success or failure in the passage of social welfare legislation emphasize certain key characteristics of our system. These are the intense conflict and rivalry of the parties, the lack of party discipline (less true today than in the past), the role and influence of special interests, and the lack of enthusiasm in the United States Congress for innovative policies to provide more health care insurance and poor relief. One key special interest with a major role in American politics, perhaps a deciding role, is Big Business.

The congressional battle in the United States on legislation to provide poor relief is both a battle between the legislative Democratic and Republican parties as well as somewhat an internal difference for each party. This can be illustrated by the roll call votes during Lyndon Johnson's presidency. When the food stamps program was voted on in Congress 86% of the Republicans in the House opposed it while only 17% of the House Democrats opposed it. In the Senate 69% of Republicans opposed it while only 20% of Democratic Senators opposed. The Republican record on such legislation since the 1930s has been largely oppositional, but there are a minority of conservative Democrats as well. We clearly need more national policy makers with more commitment to deal humanely and effectively with the relief needs of the poor. One final, but very significant point: in midterm elections, between presidential elections, when the United States Congress is up for election, the voter turnout is low, during the past 30 years. Thus, over 60% of American eligible voters stay home in these elections. This is because they are too busy, unconcerned that it makes a difference, have a loss of confidence in the Congress and/or feel that they will not, and have not, benefited from the action of their representative. They have no sense of civic duty, no desire to be involved. And their parties fail to mobilize them. This is quite different than in Europe where parliamentary elections attract 70% or more of the voters.

Reviewing this history one realizes how difficult, how infrequent, it is to mobilize a humane majority in Congress to adopt anti-poverty legislation. One realizes how the Congress is less open and less representative of the needs and interests of the "underclass" in American society. This is the basic finding of Sidney Verba and Norman Nie on "representation" in the United States and other democracies. Their study suggests strongly that in the United States legislative leaders take policy positions which, are more "concurrent" with the views of those constituents with a higher socioeconomic status and with those constituents who are more politically active, than is the case in Europe. [12] This raises the basic question—are our legislative leaders genuinely concerned about, and representative of, the poor, the needy, the destitute? In Western Europe they have a record of more humane representation.

Notes

1. See Robert D. Putnam, *The Comparative Study of Political Elites* (Englewood Cliffs, NJ: Prentice Hall, 1976), 22-23, 177-187.

2. Joel D. Aberbach, Robert D. Putnam and Bert A. Rockman, *Bureaucrats and Politicians in Western Democracies* (Cambridge, MA: Harvard University Press, 1981), 60.

3. Two sources are used for these data: Gary C. Jacobson, *The Politics of Congressional Elections* (New York: Longman 2000) and Gerald M. Pomper et al, *The Election of 2000: Reports and Interpretations*, (New York: Chatham House, 2001), 99, 106, 111, 112, 117, 119.

4. Herbert E. Alexander, ed., *Comparative Political Finance in the 1980s* (New York: Cambridge University Press, 1989), 31, 206; for the United States see Samuel J. Eldersveld and Hanes Walton, Jr., *Political Parties in American Society* (Boston: Bedford/St. Martin's), 255, 258.

5. Rudy B. Andeweg and Galen A. Irwin, *Dutch Government and Politics*, (London: the Macmillan Press, 1993), 95-96.

6. Harold W. Stanley and Richard G. Niemi, *Vital Statistics on American Politics*, (Washington, DC: Congressional Quarterly Press, 1995), 187-188.

7. Data is taken from Table 1 of William Crotty, John S. Jackson III, and Melissa K. Miller, "Political Activists Over Time: Working Elites' in the Party System"; in Birol Yesilada, ed. *Comparative Political Parties and Party Elites* (Ann Arbor, MI: University of Michigan Press, 1999), 266-275. A chi-square test on the tabular data in Table 5.1 shows the differences between Republican delegate and Democratic delegate support for social-welfare services as well as support for government insurance are very highly statistically significant ($p < 0.001$ for both). Delegate data was collected by John S. Jackson, III while the party follower data was obtained from the American National Election Studies Cumulative Data File, 1952-1992. Delegate data consists of both delegates to the 1992 Republican National Convention ($n = 369$) and delegates to the 1992 Democratic National Convention ($n = 506$). Follower data was from respondents who identified themselves as either "strong" or "weak" identifiers with the Republican party (n=623) as well as respondents who identified themselves

as either "strong" or "weak" identifiers with the Democratic party (n=879).

8. Hugh Bochel, *Parliament and Welfare Policy* (Aldershot, England: Dartmouth, 1992), 23, 54.

9. Galen A. Irwin and Jacques Thomassen, "Issue Consensus in a Multiparty System: Voters and Leaders in the Netherlands," *Acta Politica*, (October, 1975), 404.

10. Nathan Miller, *FDR an Intimate History* (Garden City: NY. Doubleday and Co., 1983), 373-375, is one of many biographies which describes these events.

11. See Theodore C. Sorensen, *Kennedy* (New York: Harper & Row, 1965), 339-345.

12. Sidney Verba and Norman H. Nie, *Participation in America* (New York: Harper, 1972), 337-340.

Chapter 6

The Business Elite's Political Role in the United States Compared to Europe

In explaining why the United States lags behind Western Europe in dealing with the poverty problem the distinctive role of the American business elite must be considered seriously. That is, frankly, our position. No doubt there are other forces and conditions—historical, or institutional, and normative which converge with the special political role of American capitalism, to explain our neglect. But the functional role of business leaders in the American process is very important, if not from time to time decisive.

Wealth and political power have always been closely linked in the story of the development of modern societies. Kevin Phillips and others have dramatically described this linkage in America in detail.[1]

Studies have used such subtitles as "the buying of the Presidency," the "buying of Congress," "the corruption of American politics." Many of them conclude their analyses of American business's role in politics with such conclusions as: "money becomes evil. . . . when it is used to buy power" (Huntington), or "when politics becomes hostage to money, as it did in the late 19th century, and as it increasingly is today, people suffer."[2]

This association between wealth and political power, however, varies considerably by country, particularly with regard to our basic substantive concern—poverty. Wealth can facilitate the adoption of policies providing relief to the poor, or wealth can be a hindrance, a major obstacle in the way of adopting such welfare policies. In our opinion, this in a general sense is a major factor, a major explanation for the relative failure of the United States' anti-poverty legislation compared to Western Europe. Thus, the major question is how differently does the American business elite function in the American political system, and how does this work out in such a way

Table 6.1: United States Congress and Occupational Background (1993)

Background	House (435)	Senate (100)
Law	42% ($n = 170$)	61%
Banking/Business	37% ($n = 164$)	31%

Source: Harold Stanley and Richard Niemi, *Vital Statistics on American Politics*, 1995, 187–188.

as to be a key causal link to the nonperformance or poor performance of the American political system in taking care of the poor? Another way perhaps to ask this is: why and how does capitalism operate so differently in Western European countries so that business participated (and participates) so supportingly in the social reform programs of these societies, both intellectually and financially, while not supportively in the United States?

The first significant difference is that in the United States the business and corporate elite are extremely wealthy, and increasingly wealthy. We are the major economic power in the world, and the wealth accumulated by United States business is awesome. We have more millionaires and billionaires than any other country.[3] And the wealthy continue to become more affluent. In 1979 the top one percent of the American population in terms of income held 22% of the nation's wealth. After the Reagan tax cuts (and other policies favoring business) in 1989 the percentage was 39%. And since then the concentration has increased. So the United States has become an increasingly inegalitarian society over the years. The poor are relatively poorer, and the rich are richer, and more of the very rich are billionaires. Today, 2006, the rich are celebrating the new Bush tax cuts again. The conception of democracy held by many of these in the business elite is that democracy must, if it is efficient, promote wealth—maximizing outcomes. That is to them the true test of the democratic system. This is not so in Europe.

The second major characteristic of this dominant and acquisitive business elite is that it seeks to influence, if not control, governmental personnel and policy. The business elite seeks to control who becomes President and how he performs in office. If not candidates for the United States Congress themselves, they seek to spend much on seeing that the "right" candidates are selected, and supports them in their campaigns, to see that they are elected. It is interesting to see from what occupations congressional leadership comes. The following table provides evidence of the success of candidates with a business or business-related background in running for and winning national office.

This close involvement with government and politics goes back to the late 19th and early 20th century. Already by 1902–3 we were electing millionaires to the United States Senate. Phillips lists 21 millionaires in that Senate (from public utilities, railroads, lumber, banking, insurance, mining, and ranching).[4] This nicely set the stage for the influence of "Big Money" on "Big Politics." We have continued this millionaires-in-Congress pattern in recent years.

The third characteristic of the business and corporate elite role in politics has been their direct funding of the political parties' campaigns. This began already in the latter part of the 19th century and has grown to incredible levels in recent election campaigns.[5] In 1860, Abraham Lincoln's election cost him and the Republicans $100,000 and Douglas, the Democratic candidate $50,000. By 1880 both parties were spending over a million, and by 1900 that had increased to $3,000,000 for the Republicans (McKinley) and $425,000 for the Democrats (Bryan). These escalating costs forced the parties to seek funds from corporations and the wealthy. The role of corporations was getting so great that in 1907 President Theodore Roosevelt persuaded Congress to pass a law forbidding corporations from contributing directly to parties or candidates. The loophole of course was that the corporate executives (and their families) could give as much money from their personal wealth as they pleased. Big names in the corporate world did make big contributions—Rockefeller, Cooke, Harriman, Carnegie, etc. The money was given to both parties, but, as Alexander notes, the idea "that businessmen should support the political party that must clearly favored their interests was accepted"—not only the Republican Party. Certain wealthy sponsors did give large sums, such as in 1904 when August Belmont and Thomas Fortune Ryan gave $700,000 to the Democrats (which took care of most of their costs for that campaign.)

Very early also these contributors to the parties expected to have access and influence. Harriman gave heavily to the Teddy Roosevelt campaign with the explicit expectation that Chauncey Depew would be appointed ambassador to France. When it didn't happen, he exploded in anger and refused any contribution in 1908. Another racy story about influence is recounted by Alexander, also in the 1908 campaign. Teddy Roosevelt was running for reelection and the costs were so high and the contributions so low that he went to two wealthy Republicans for help—Harriman and Henry C. Frick, a partner of Andrew Carnegie. Frick reported later that Teddy begged for financial support. Frick reported this occasion as follows: "He got down on his knees to us. We bought the son of a bitch, and then he did not stay bought!"[6] This is somewhat reminiscent of a claim by a business contributor in the 2000 election who allegedly excitedly and jubilantly told his friends "now we are going to be in the Oval office." Despite all our attempts to regulate campaign contributions and expenditures, particularly since Watergate, this same dominant quid-pro-quo attitude of Big Money in American elections remains. As we reported earlier, in 2000 almost two billion dollars were spent on the national elections. Who has that kind of money in the United States?—the wealthy, the affluent, the corporate and business elite.

These three features of the way the business elite have functioned in the American system are strikingly different from the West European systems. There is much less wealth, personal or corporate, associated with the parties in Europe. Further, there is no conception or motivation by business in these countries to dominate the political system. And so far as influencing elections is concerned, business does not define its role in these terms. In a system like the Netherlands, for example, in recent elections, as we explained in our earlier discussion of campaigns, the campaign expenditures are very limited. Very limited funds are spent on purchasing broadcasting time. Party membership dues pay for a large part of these costs. Some additional funds are solicited by the national organizations of the parties, but these are not large, and "almost nothing comes explicitly from business." [7] Similar generalizations can be made about the role of money in election campaigns in other countries. Business plays no significant role as in the United States.

The relevance of a strong, if not a towering, role of business in the American system for the adoption of social welfare legislation, particularly anti-poverty legislation, must become clearer now. With all this desire for influence and all these resources, as well as all the opportunities, for playing a major role in government, one might (perhaps foolishly) hope that the role of the business elite would be progressive, even liberal. But that is not the case. The studies of business leaders' attitudes reveal them as conservative, much more so than in other Western systems. In a comparative study of elites (governmental, business, party, labor, and farm) Verba and his colleagues at Harvard found that the United States business elites differed substantially from those in Sweden or Japan. Two questions were put to these elites on social welfare: (1) government aid for the elderly and handicapped and (2) government provision of welfare benefits and government-guaranteed jobs to the needy. Compared to Sweden, United States business leaders scored negatively on both questions. The findings for business leaders specifically were:[8]

% Favoring Government aid/provision for	Sweden	United States	Japan
1. Old and handicapped	65%	48%	35%
2. Welfare services to needy	55%	15%	60%

Verba concluded "The Swedish conservative and business leaders are far more supportive of the welfare state than their American colleagues."[9] In this study the United States business leaders ranked close to Republican leaders on both scales. In another study of American elites (12 categories 1,830 total number) it was reported that when business leaders were asked their ideological position 63% replied "conservative" and only 14% "liberal."[10] This confirms what we would expect, that American business elites have a position ideologically close to the Republicans. American business elites today still believe strongly in the free market, the pursuit of more wealth, and a belief in limited government unless it is needed to help business maximize its wealth. They are ardent admirers of Adam Smith who in 1776 laid down this doctrine in his book, The Wealth of Nations. What they never read, nor quote, from Adam Smith is a lengthy essay he wrote on "the theory of Moral Sentiment" in which he also said the following.

> The wise and virtuous man is at all times willing that his own private interest should be sacrificed to the public interest of his own particular order of society. He is at all times willing, too, that the interest of this order of society should be sacrificed to the greater interest of the state."[11]

The more we study the capitalist system in the United States and how it functions, and the American business elite and how, on what principles, it functions, the more we realize that this is a differently acting capitalist system than in the countries of Western Europe. Our business elite is often an obstacle to social welfare programs, whereas the business elite in Europe contribute willingly to support social welfare reform and the provision of relief to all their poor.[12]

Historically big business has been skeptical of government efforts to care for the underclass. The case of the Roosevelt presidency illustrates this. When the depression of 1929 forced governmental action eventually, which indeed occurred with Franklin Roosevelt's election in 1932, big business did little to support FDR's program. As one of his biographers put it, Roosevelt "was contemptuous of bankers and big businessmen who had been discredited by their inability to deal with the depression."[13] FDR sought immediately to deal with demoralizing problems which Americans faced, enacting the NIRA, to help industry, AAA to help agriculture, WPA and NYA to give the unemployed jobs, etc. He asserted at the time when he was crafting the Social Security Act of 1935 that "there is no reason why everybody in the United States should not be covered."[14] He was warned, however, that such a broad and sweeping social welfare reform would be difficult to get through Congress. And thus had to cut down the eligibility under the old age pension section of the law to only one-fourth of the oldsters who should be included. He also was warned not to push for national health insurance at that time because it would not pass (the AMA was strong and would defeat it.) Business gave minimal and grudging support to FDR's program, if they supported it at all. Henry Ford announced early that he would not comply with the NIRA regulations, true also for other businesses. And in May, 1935 the United States Chamber of Commerce at its annual meeting denounced the president's program. Roosevelt antagonized business with his policies, particularly when he presented his tax reform legislative proposals. American business leaders opposed Roosevelt throughout his presidency. They felt that his "Keynesian" programs had failed, and wanted less government and tax cuts–this was the way to end a recession. This of course sounds very familiar today!

One of the major differences between the government strategy and role of the American business elite and the business elites' strategy and role in Western European systems is that American business has never acted as a partner with labor and government to solve the problems of the needy in our societies. In West European systems the basic conception of how business should, and does, get involved in the policy process is different. The Dutch, Scandinavian, and Belgium systems are "neo-corporative" systems, as they are called. Business is consulted by the government along with other interest groups, and enters actively into the bargaining process by which decisions are arrived at. But business is not the dominant interest, it does not penetrate government, it does not finance the recruitment of the legislative members or administrators, it does not control the decisions made. In the Netherlands, for example, there are "advisory councils" for types of policy areas (health, environment, social welfare, etc.), as well as advisory councils for ministries. At the peak of the system is a body called the Social Economic Council (SER) made up of 45 persons (15 from business, 15 from labor, and 15 appointed by the government on behalf of the Queen, called "Crown" members). This group deliberates and bargains and finally arrives at a proposed solution to a particular policy issue. This proposed solution is then sent to the Cabinet and the Parliament for final action. In this context business (which has its own organization of employers) has to reason with and compromise its position at two levels of the system.[15] One should be aware that recently in the Netherlands (2003) this system of councils and SER has been criticized as too consensual, and is in process of revision by the government. This system emerged after World War II particularly as a result of discussions in Holland in the "underground" during the war, among business leaders and labor leaders and intellectuals who were deliberating over what type of government they wanted when the war was over.

In sharp contrast to this "neo-corporatist" model is the "corporate dominance" model in the United States. The corporate and business elite do not operate through a deliberative institutional system on equal terms with labor and other interest groups. Rather the business elite in the United

States seeks to influence, if not control, government by having major influence in one, if not both, of the parties, and thus to have major influence in Congress, as well as the presidency, by recruiting "satisfactory" candidates and purchasing "access" if not "control" during the campaigns and later when their candidates take office. Given what we know about the costs of running for office in the United States, and the attitudes of the upper income groups toward welfare policies, and the social backgrounds and wealth of our Republican (and Democratic) congressmen and congresswomen, and their deep desires to be reelected—the consequences are obvious. The corporationist model of the role of business in politics is an extreme antithesis to the Western European model of business partnership with politicians. And this American model can be frightfully successful in keeping truly inclusive anti-poverty legislation off the agenda of Congress.

We must keep in mind here that we are trying to explain why in the United States there is so much poverty compared to Western Europe, and so much less relief of the poor. The role of business is only one (but major) factor in the equation. We do not mean to say it is the primary cause, and we have already indicated other relevant factors. Nor do we mean to completely malign American business for its role in this matter. We certainly are aware of the benefits of American capitalism, for the development of our industrial system and the improvement of economic and social conditions of life, as well as the opportunities for a better life for many people. But capitalism has had its deleterious effects in America—our slums, ghettos, the shelterless, the food kitchens and pantries, the uncared for children on the streets, the destitute ill, the millions without health insurance, the people sleeping on the streets, the poverty—even among those who do work. The capitalist elites in America often ignore these miseries. That is not to say that they are not philanthropic or charitable. Setting up foundations, building libraries, music theatres, even schools. But that doesn't take care of our problem. As we noted earlier, corporations contribute only a small percentage (less than 10%) to the 200 billion dollars of charitable contributions each year. Obviously caring for our poor is still an unmet responsibility which only our government can meet, hopefully with the assistance of humane business leaders in politics.

Notes

1. Kevin P. Phillips, *Wealth and Democracy: A Political History of the American Rich* (New York: Broadway Books, 2002).

2. Phillips, *Wealth and Democracy*, xiv, xv.

3. For an elaborate description of wealth in the United States see Phillips, *Wealth and Democracy*.

4. Phillips, *Wealth and Democracy*, 240. See also the study of the Senate by Donald R. Matthews, *United States Senators and Their World* (New York: Norton, 1973). He reports on 53 Senators (17 Democratic, 36 Republican) in the 1956 Senate.

5. Herbert E. Alexander, *Financing Politics: Money, Elections and Political Reform* (Washington, D.C., Congressional Quarterly Press, 1976).

6. Alexander, *Financing Politics*, 66.

7. Rudy Andeweg and Galen Irwin, *Dutch Government and Politics* (London: the Macmillan Press, 1993), 95–96.

8. Sidney Verba and Steven Kelman, *Elites and the Idea of Equality: A Comparison of Japan, Sweden and the United States* (Cambridge, MA.: Harvard University Press, 1987), 75. The data are based on interviews with 299 business leaders in Japan, 912 in Sweden, and 312 in the United States. These percentages are adapted from the data presented in this study.

9. Verba, *Elites and the Idea of Equality*, 76.

10. Robert Lerner, Althea Nagai and Stanley Rothman, *American Elites* (New Haven: Yale University Press, 1996), 50.

11. Adam Smith, *An Inquiry into the Nature and Causes of the Wealth of Nations* (London, W. Strahan and T. Cadell (1776).

12. See Chapter 3 where we discuss the attitudes of American business leaders in the 19th century, particularly their opposition to caring for the poor.

13. Nathan Miller, *FDR: An Intimate History* (Garden City, NY, Doubleday and Co., 1983), 327.

14. Miller, *FDR: An Intimate History*, 373.

15. For a description of their system see Andeweg and Irwin, *Dutch Government and Politics*, 164–168.

Part II

Historical Studies of Poverty in the United States, the Netherlands, Britain, France, Belgium, Germany and Sweden

Chapter 7

Early American History of Poverty

In seeking today to explain our poverty problem, a knowledge of our historical experience—how Americans long ago viewed poverty and how they sought to deal with it—may be very relevant. Did we take a collective, or individualist, approach in the past? What was the role of the church and of private charity? To what extent were public funds provided for the relief of the poor? Above all, what was the basic norm concerning social and governmental responsibility in caring for the poor which emerged during our historical development? These and other specific questions can be answered on the basis of historical scholarship.

There are two major ways in which the relevance of history can be discussed in our poverty analysis. One is to see our strategies and ways of characterizing poverty today as traceable to a long history of particular experiences. That is, to see a path from the past, perhaps as early as the 17th century in New England, to the present. The position might be taken that we early viewed poverty from a particular social, political, or even moral perspective and over time have become socialized to the acceptance of that perspective, even today. Just as we are inclined to trace certain elements of American democratic belief today to our experiences in the latter part of the 18th century.

On the other hand we may, in reviewing the history of the treatment of the poor in early America, reject the idea of historical continuity. We may then argue that our present approaches in some respects at least, constitute a rejection of the past approach to poverty as unacceptable or unworkable, that a basic disconnect has occurred. Our liberalization of the franchise in the 19th century and the 20th century may provide an example of how change in norms and practices can occur over time. In a sense we may perceive two "cultures of poverty", one in the 17th and 18th centuries and a second culture of poverty today.

In this historical review we focus analytically on certain key aspects of the historical experience. Obviously, we looked at the extent of poverty and how it changed over time, how it varied by locale, from city to city, and what might explain these variations. Next we were interested in the attitudes of people toward poverty, particularly the view of the middle and upper classes. Did they accept it sympathetically or not? Did they try to distinguish between the deserving and undeserving poor? Was there a sense of social responsibility for caring for the poor? Did leaders and the public share their views or disagree? Politically was there a community consensus (leaders and public), or was there significant disagreement, among political leaders and between political leaders and the merchants (or the business elites) in these early communities? In a sense were there something like cultural normative orientations emerging in people's views of poverty and how to deal with it? In this connection, what were the views of the church leaders, of both traditional and liberal churches on the moral and spiritual (biblical) issues in helping the poor? In all of this, of course, we are interested in the role that institutions played—local government, (eventually the national government), churches, and charitable groups, and also the media. New England cities in the early years already had democratic elections (though often influenced by British governors), active city councils, and local bureaucracies administering the laws. What roles did they play in working out solutions to the poverty problem? A variety of theories have been advanced by recent students of American poverty and our treatment of the poor today—emphasizing institutions, or culture norms, or leadership behavior. It is interesting to see how these played a role historically in the context of actions to resolve poverty questions in those days.

Early Studies of New England Cities

We are indebted to historians who have studied in detail cities like Boston, New York, and Philadelphia from the late 17th century to the Revolution. Their examination of the city records for all residents and the tax rolls are very informative.[1] These were small towns in that period up to 1700—the population of Boston was 6,000, New York 4,500, and Philadelphia 2,200. They each had their own governments with city councils, justice of the peace, mayors, functioning of course under the constraints of English rule. Already in this early period there was stratification of the city in terms of wealth and political status. In Boston (and New York and Philadelphia) an examination of economic status based on taxable assets revealed a 4-tiered system. At the bottom were the 30% who owned only 3% of the community's assets; at the next, higher, level another 30% with 11% of the wealth; a third level also of 30% with 40% of the assets; and the rich 10% at the top controlling 45% to 50% of total community assets.

The poor consisted of laborers, seamen, carpenters, shoemakers, widows (Boston particularly was known as a city with many poor widows), and of course the elderly unable to work, the disabled, the ill and unemployables. The exact number of poor was hard to determine because there did not exist anything like a "poverty line" as we have today, specifying the income necessary to live at a minimum level of comfort. Further, the number of the poor fluctuated greatly, depending on economic circumstances, epidemics, and wars. In 1676 the war in Massachusetts when the Native American tribes attacked the frontier settlements resulted in droves of settlers arriving in Boston to seek help. And the expedition against Quebec in 1690 which ended in disaster for the colonists of Massachusetts left many widows and orphans needing poor relief. Estimates of the exact poverty thus varied over time. Normally, in times of peace and relative economic stability the amount of poverty was low, but the potential was always high, especially for the 30% at the lower level of economy whose assets were so minimal they were not required to pay taxes. Later, as we follow these cities in the 18th century the incidence of poverty was much greater. One study of Boston reported that from 30% to 40% of the citizens of Boston by 1771 (by then a city of 20,000) were in a state of poverty or "near poverty." Income inequality also increased during this period as follows:[2]

Percentage of Wealth Held (Boston)			
Wealth Level	1687	1771	1790
Bottom 30%	2.5	0.1	0.03
Low Middle 30%	11.3	9.4	4.8
Upper Middle 30%	39.6	27.0	30.5
Top 10%	46.6	63.5	64.7
Top 1%	9.5	26.0	27.1

How did the colonists deal with the problem of poverty? In the early period before 1700 it was apparently viewed as a "familial" and community problem. As Nash reports "little stigma was attached to poverty" because it was not the fault of the individual. Further, he says, after the poverty in Boston increased to "unprecedented proportions" following the disastrous defeat at Quebec, the city's dwellers "regarded poor relief as a communal responsibility."[3] The cities collected and spent tax money on poor relief. In New York legislation was passed in 1683 directing local officials to "make provisions for the maintenance and support of the poor." In Philadelphia the law required justices of the peace to take care of the needs of the indigent.[4]

After 1700 there was a gradual increase in the number of the poor, although its incidence rose and fell with economic conditions and epidemic crises (such as yellow fever). The poor were cared for by what was called out-relief, providing food and other necessities to individuals in their homes. The tax burdens for poor relief increased (to 600 English pounds in Boston by 1742). Church wardens provided relief in New York while the city's overseers of the poor did so in Boston. As the burden of poverty increased, New England towns looked for new approaches to the problem. Almshouses had already existed before 1700. They were now used primarily to take care of the elderly, sick, disabled and mentally retarded. Boston turned to the idea of the "workhouse", under a law passed in 1735. This was built on Boston Commons and was in use by 1741. It was used to house unemployed but also able poor who worked on various trades, such as weaving cloth, making shoes, etc.

Other strategies were developed for dealing with poverty particularly in Boston, where it had become a "major social problem." One practice was started to deal with the children of poor families. The practice was called "binding out." It provided for putting the children of the poor in homes of the well-to-do, virtually as indentured servants. Thus the costs of caring for the children of the poor, the responsibility of the overseers of the poor, were eliminated. By the 1740s 178 children were bound over.[5] Another practice was called "warning out." This was a way of reducing the poverty burden by informing new arrivals in the city that they would not be eligible for poor relief. By exclusion of these refugees and vagrants, basically because they did not meet residential requirements, many poor were refused aid. This practice began in 1745 in Boston. Each warning by overseers of the poor was recorded. In the first five years there were almost 400 such cases, by the 1790s almost 2,500.[6]

As poor relief costs increased Boston leaders turned to charity, asking for greater contributions from the wealthy. They also appealed to the General Court for tax relief, a request which was rejected. Further, in Boston the public workhouse movement had taken hold. The large building on Boston Commons was operating—50 persons were pressured to go and work there. There was, however, considerable reluctance to go to the workhouse, and many refused outright. The proposal was then made to have a "linen manufactory" for poverty stricken widows, with the idea that women would weave and make linens which could then be sold at a profit. This opened in 1751 and did produce much linen. However, despite urgings from city leaders and religious authorities, support declined. And the merchandise produced was not adequate to support it either. So the "linen manufactory" closed in 1755. It closed because it could not produce cloth cheaply enough.

A final major effort to put the poor to work, involving local political leaders and the business elite, was launched in Boston, New York and Philadelphia. It was linked to the nonimportation (of English goods) movement. "Manufactories" employed poor people to make sail cloth as well as other goods. In Boston a committee was set up and authorized to put such a plan into effect. In Philadelphia the Quakers turned over to the merchants the running of their "Bettering House" with all but 15% of poor relief money channeled to that institution. Eventually all these efforts were criticized, overseers of the poor opposed it, not enough of the poor participated, the merchants did not profit enough, and taxpayers were disillusioned. By 1775 these efforts failed. Only public tax support for the poor remained.

As one reviews this century of early American history, it is important to remember certain key patterns. There was obviously considerable poverty, increasing from 1740 on. There was an early sense of social, community and political responsibility for dealing with the poverty problem. Local government was the key actor. True, there were limits (on outsiders) and preference for supporting particular groups, such as widows and orphans, but there was a basic acceptance of the need to care for other poor also. The church played a role, through charity, but the central actor was the local council and its overseers of the poor. A variety of strategies and approaches were taken—almshouses, workhouses, linen manufactories, as well as "outdoor relief" at the home—but in the last analysis it was the taxpayer who was the provider, aided by familial and church charity and some wealthy benefactors. The 30% to 40% at the lower economic status level of these cities were constantly in a struggle to survive. Many could not make it. It was the government who from the beginning in the 1600s seemed to accept that the provision for poor relief was its role, even though it complained at the cost.

There was an ideological conflict at the elite level—particularly on the basic question of whether government should provide for relief. Benjamin Franklin wrote in 1766 "the more public provisions were made for the poor, the less they provided for themselves and of course became poorer. And, on the contrary, the less was done for them, the more they did for themselves, and became richer."[7] It is interesting that the Philadelphia leaders did not accept Franklin's advice. This self-help argument had some roots at least in the beliefs of some of the Puritans. Rev. Cotton Mather wrote in 1721 "for those who indulge themselves in idleness, the Express Command of God unto us, (is) that you should let them starve."[8] And the Boston clergyman Chauncy in 1752 used in his sermon this text: "this we commanded you, that if any would not work, neither should he eat."[9] He warned against giving money to the poor, because "charity of this kind, far from helping, would be a great hurt to a community."

There were, however, preachers who were more "liberal." There was considerable radical political evangelism during that middle period of the Seventies. George Whitefield preached to large crowds in these New England cities, in churches and in the open air to 20,000 in Boston Commons one Saturday. He attacked the wealthy class and urged the masses to "seek their own salvation." Although at first he was welcomed by the city fathers because they thought he would usher in a new period of morality and social peace. But as they listened to this preacher they became more and more worried. He criticized other preachers and traditional religion generally. Whitefield was followed by other radical itinerant preachers. Gilbert Tennent was one who preached social egalitarianism. And he was followed by James Davenport in 1742 who was refused the pulpits of all the Boston churches, because he accused the clergy of being corrupt and unconverted while he praised "God's people", the poor dispossessed. Davenport attacked the rich and powerful, saw the yawning gap between the rich and the poor. So provoked was Rev. Charles Chauncy of the First Church in Boston that he denounced such radical revelation as attempting to destroy all property, to make things common, "wives as well as goods." With such rousing evangelism the basis was laid for mass agitation and protest, and set in motion the actions of the masses repugnant to the well-to-do. Large revivalist crowds gathered, formed street parades, repeated threats to those in authority, and sparked a revolutionary spirit. The role of the masses and their health and welfare had become a very divisive issue.

Poverty in the Later 18th and Early 19th Centuries

The period from 1770 to the close of the century is interesting, particularly to assess the poverty problem before and after the war of Independence. Kulikoff analyzed the conditions in Boston during this period. He estimates that 30% to 40% of the population from 1770 to 1790 were destitute, based on records of widows, unemployed, blacks, poorly paid artisans and those in the poor house.[10] He noticed that segregation and concentration of the poor had occurred, in two outlying districts of Boston. The data revealed an increasing inequality of wealth with only three percent of city wealth held by the bottom third of the population. What is particularly troublesome, in contrast to the earlier periods of Boston's history, is that the elites in Boston did not manifest much social responsibility toward the poor. "Noblesse oblige was practically nonexistent", Kulikoff claims.[11] The main exception to this were the widows who were helped, otherwise there were only minimal bequests and funds from the city or from charities which were distributed by the overseers of the poor. There was considerable population mobility in Boston during this late 18th century period—many new immigrants from abroad, as well as travelers looking for jobs, and also some occupational mobility within the city. Obviously this meant an unstable labor force, a great deal of "warning out" of people who the city did not want to support, and less sense of a community taking care of the unemployed and poor.

The state of poverty and its relief in New York City and its rural environs was quite different during the 18th century and early 19th centuries. Cray's study presents in great detail this period, not only for the city but for the surrounding counties (Queens, Suffolk, and Westchester). This history of New York City demonstrates the complex character of the poverty problem in those days and also the varied approaches by which the city and town leaders sought to deal with it, during the pre-revolutionary period, and the period leading to the war of 1812.[12] The rural areas used more informal approaches; the city relied heavily on institutional relief. The almshouse evolved from a very limited refuge for the marginalized elderly, sick, and retarded elements, to eventually a structure which was at the same time a workhouse for the unemployed, as well as a factory which produced goods for sale, as was the case for the Bellevue almshouse of 1816. This three story building was a great advance over earlier versions.

Other innovations were introduced. The worst perhaps were the "pauper auctions", similar to slave or indentured servant sales. While home relief (or "out relief") continued for those poor who would not, or could not, leave their homes, apprenticeships of the children of the poor continued. Further, badging was adopted at one point, so a poor person could be identified, and certified in a sense: a variation of this was the "passport system." Church relief was also sought by the overseer of the poor, from the Dutch Reformed, the Quakers, the other Protestant churches, as well as the French (Catholics, presumably). As poverty increased, financial appeals for assistance increased, the poor tax levy increased, and at one time the local officials sought to coerce the former employers of the poor (as well as any relatives of the poor) to contribute. Sometimes "transportation" of certain poor out of the city was also done.

Thus, the key features of the system were: local government assumed responsibility, churches were involved to the extent possible, and officials desperately looked for other ways to handle demands on them, looking particularly for ways of controlling costs. It was usually a compassionate system of direct governmental aid with rigorous controls built into it from time to time. There were often complaints about the system from various types of persons. The superintendent of the almshouse himself was critical, noting abuses (such as "double dipping") and partisan leaders sometimes suggested reforms, often rejected. The established almshouse system remained the center of the relief effort in New York.

Economic conditions, such as the panic of 1819, as well as the increased needs of the poor, resulted in the rising costs. Charitable expenditures, for example, increased from $46,000 in 1807 to $78,000 in 1809.[13] The almshouse was overcrowded. In addition the poor were often organizing protests for more assistance. While counties were not in a state of crisis, Manhattan gradually became more pressed for new solutions. At one point one writer concludes that this period of trial in New York reflected a change in values. "Increasingly the values of the market place infiltrated the basic structure of public charity." And, again, "these changes in public charity reflected alterations within the society itself as the last vestiges of the moral economy crumbled before the unfettered competition of the market place." As the 19th century unfolded, the large question is—was the ideology of the free market place indeed taking over?[14]

One key aspect of this developing poor relief system was that some business leaders were playing a role. After all, there was a close correlation between wealth and political status. Many of the aldermen, selectmen, overseers of the poor, church wardens and vestrymen were persons with businesses. It is true that one does not read often in these historical descriptions that business leaders took the lead, but sometimes they did (as the merchants in Boston united behind the establishment of a new workhouse). And it is also true that some wealthy business people as Puritans adhered to the Cotton Mather negative ideology about poverty. Yet, most business leaders did not subscribe, at least not openly, to such warped biblical interpretations. In short, many business leaders worked in Boston and New York City in government or through government to implement some type of helpful poverty relief system.

Scholars reviewing our success (and failures) in dealing with poverty up to 1830[15] comment on persisting tendencies. The distinction between deserving and undeserving poor was used early and continued. Poor persons were not automatically taken care of; indeed, many seemed to be forced to work out their own life solutions. There was the "warnings out" approach, the occasional "transportation" of undesirables out of town. And not everyone was admitted to the almshouse or poor house (and many also refused to go to these institutions and yet could not get "out relief"). On the other hand there was a strong sense of obligation to the deserving poor. The creation of institutions to cope with poverty was also clearly established, though changed somewhat in the 19th century. "Poor" institutions became more "narrow" in function—special places for the elderly, for the mentally retarded, hospitals for the sick, jails for the criminal element. The evidence of a "culture of poverty" emerged but changed somewhat over time. Poverty was sometimes associated with idleness, alcohol, petty crime, inability to hold a job when given one, squandering of resources and (eventually) use of drugs. Finally, a major continuity was the assumption of governmental action by the city, although in the 19th century in some areas the county gradually took over more of the poverty relief role.

Thus we had a fairly clear line of historical development from the 17th century on, as to the roles of government and church in socio-economic help to the poor. And also a clear line in attitudes toward the poor, differentiations among the poor, and variations in strategies to use with the different types of poor. This historical body of data is important to keep in mind in viewing the problems of the poor in the last half of the 19th century and the 20th century. It is important to keep asking which of these features persisted and which of them were superseded in the subsequent evolution of our poor relief system, and why and with what consequences? Also, one could ask, which approaches were never attempted—in the early American history?

One must remember that in 1789 we adopted our constitution providing for a new system of government, structurally democratic, ideologically committed to equality, federal in the distribution of national and state powers, and bolstered by a lengthy Bill of Rights. By 1800 already we saw the emergence of a two-party system: the Federalists and the Republicans (later the Democrats) embroiled in partisan competition which was sharp and often bitter. Coping with this system affected strategies of policy advocates. Particularly the elites at the state and local levels dealing with the poverty question had to cope also. Under this structure not much was attempted at the national level in dealing with the poverty problem, until after the Civil War. In the meantime, however, the ideological controversy over capitalism was significant for our eventual efforts to deal with poverty nationally.

The Controversy Over the Poverty Role of Government

From the middle of the 18th century on and to the end of the 19th century there was a great and continual clash of beliefs over the proper role of the government. Statesmen, clergy, philosophers, and academicians were deeply involved in this. Perhaps in the decade before the Revolutionary War the ideas of the "patriot" statesmen began this debate. Samuel Adams, John Adams, Patrick Henry, Thomas Paine and others wrote (and spoke) of the natural laws above the state as well as the inalienable rights of the individual which government had to respect. The colonists' increasing hostility to their English governors certainly played a big role in the onset of these beliefs. Later, Adam Smith's the Wealth of Nations (1776) developed the argument in economic terms.[16] Upset by English mercantilist policies against the colonists, Smith argued for an economic life free from governmental intervention; "every man. . . . should be free to pursue his own interest his own way." Other scholars followed Smith with their expansion of this concept. So far as poverty was concerned they said that the poor must realize "that they are themselves the cause of their own poverty, that the means of redress are in their own hands. . . . "[17] These laissez-faire economic theorists denounced poor laws and any form of poor relief.

After Independence the controversy over the proper role of the state reemerged in the battle between the leaders of the two main parties. Jefferson's Republicans argued for limited government, particularly limited federal assertions of the right to legislate on many matters, and Hamilton's

Federalists asserted the necessity for more central governmental action. The debate was manifest, for example in the question of establishing a national bank, which Jefferson opposed, as did Andrew Jackson in the 1830s, while Hamilton argued strongly for it. The Jefferson forces won this battle at the time.

The debate continued with prominent academic scholars playing a key role. One was William G. Sumner, the able sociologist at Yale who wrote at length and taught his students ardently the doctrine of laissez-faire. He was known as "the archenemy of social reform." He opposed any state action to alleviate the hardships of existence. He asserted: "let every man be sober, industrious, prudent and wise and bring up his children to be so likewise, and poverty will be abolished in a few generations."[18]

After the Civil War the debate was joined by those who were critical of laissez-faire and argued for a more positive role by the state. The religious leaders took up the cause arguing that industrialism had produced a great many problems which could only be solved by state intervention. One prominent clergyman, Washington Gladden, of the Congregational denomination, preached, and wrote, and lectured at great length in the 1870s to the 1890s, condemning the evils of capitalism. He thought the church should play a major role in "the overthrow of classical political economy." While not supporting socialism he advocated a number of state actions to promote the general welfare. He felt government should aid "the humblest and poorest and weakest."[19] Other leaders went further and embraced socialism. Indeed a Society of Christian Socialists was formed, as was a Christian Labor Union. They proposed a variety of specific reforms: provision for technical education, public employment for the unemployed, municipal public housing, slum clearance projects, and others.[20]

One should pause a moment and reflect that while these debates were raging, sometimes with considerable bitterness, the local governments in many states were continuing with their attempts to actually deal with poverty, which was a reality throughout the 19th century. They were taxing people to pay the costs of assistance to the poor, creating and administering poor houses and workhouses, and engaging in other poor relief strategies. No research has indicated that poor relief at the local level was abandoned or abated by local authorities. It is true that the national government was too preoccupied during this period to directly address the problem of poverty. There were social reform laws passed at the state level, however, such as "anti-sweat shop" laws, labor bureaus were set up in several states, mine safety legislation was adopted, there was much improvement of public education including the establishing of state boards of education, boards and commissions to supervise charities were created, and the building of some reformatories to care for "the unfit", and, finally, pensions were provided for the blind. The most relevant and significant federal laws passed were the 8-hour day (1868 and a much improved law in 1892). An 1892 Act appropriated $20,000 to investigate city slums. In 1898 an anti-sweat shop law was passed, as well as the first child labor law. But no basic national laws were passed in such social reform areas, as pensions, unemployment compensation, health insurance or poor relief.

Thus, in the latter part of the 18th century and during the 19th century it was obvious we had much experience with poverty and much debate over the role of government in dealing with poverty. Only minimal action had been taken at the national level to face up to the questions and needs of social reform. A big question never really raised was: when would our national government take responsibility for the alleviation of poverty? And what would the national government do when, if ever, it developed a conscience about poverty? Would we really see a positive role by Washington, or would we succumb to a laissez-faire ideology about poverty—a policy of inaction, lack of commitment, a rejection of national responsibility?

Veterans Benefits in the 19th Century

The United States federal government had no interest in addressing the poverty problem per se in the 19th century. But national leaders did legislate considerable funds to aid veterans and their families. This was true for the veterans of the American Revolution to some extent, although this aid was a long time coming. The Continental Congress very early expressed the intention to provide benefits to those experiencing disability, but there were no payments until 1836. This was a minimal and very belated public provision–many veterans had passed away, the average age of survivors (33,425 men) in 1832 was 74! Nevertheless, it was a first recognition of the need to reward persons for military service, and only secondarily was the motivation one of taking care of some of the needy poor. (There was one exception to this–the 1818 Act required the disabled to prove poverty before they could draw a benefit).[21] During and after the Civil War the care of union veterans and their widows and families was quite a different story. In this bloody conflict over 2 million Union soldiers fought, with over 600,000 casualties (365,000 killed). The United States Congress in Washington began adopting legislation to provide for these veterans and their families. The law specified that the amount of the payment was to be linked to the seriousness of the injury (seriously wounded lieutenant colonels $30 a month, privates $8 a month). Widows were also recognized early as deserving benefits.[22] This legislation was improved, becoming more generous as the war continued, and more costly. Veterans who were survivors received pensions. These persons, and widow benefits, increased from 10,700 in 1862 (costing $1,000,000 per year) to 126,722 by 1866 (costing $15.5 million). And of course these costs extended into the 20th century. By 1910 one-half million veterans were still on pensions (receiving an average $189 a year), and 300,000 widows were also receiving benefits. Skocpol calculates that from 1880 to 1910 the federal government allocated nearly a quarter of its expenditures to these pensions. Almost 28% of all American men aged 65 or over received United States government benefits. [23] How and why did this occur? First it was obviously a generosity based on gratitude, an emotional response to the war efforts of the soldiers. It was directed at a special interest group, really Union solders and their families, adopted by a Union Congress. It was not designed to remedy the conditions of poverty in the land generally. Veterans groups and supporters no doubt pressured for such action. But as Skocpol argues this was an action by Northern politicians, prominently the Republican leaders in the Congress in Washington. She sees it as an example of "patronage politics" in the United States in the 19th century. This is one way to characterize it surely. The assumption is that the politicians saw this in utilitarian terms, as helping their party to win in the next election. And this assumes in turn that this vote, the "veterans vote", was sizeable enough, if it was mobilized, to be influential. It is true that the electorate in the 1870s to the 1900s was relatively small–no women could vote, and the blacks were essentially excluded from the vote in the South. But turnout in presidential elections was high. According to the Bureau of the Census the turnouts were 85% in 1876, 77% in 1884, 79% in 1896. Skocpol feels that after the Reconstruction in the South (terminated in 1877), "the Republicans became locked in tight national level competition with a revived Democratic party for control of the presidency and Congress." [24] She feels that since the Republicans conceived and carried out the Civil War benefits program, the expansion of pensioners and pension costs soon worked differentially to the "advantage of the Republican party."[25] The argument is an interesting one. It assumes that pension policy was linked to perceptions of partisan advantage and vote-maximization strategies. One would like to know much more about the thinking of party elites in Congress at the time of the passage of this legislation. One motivation may have been winning the next election. But the motivation of helping the needy per se may have been more dominant for some elites, particularly in the early legislation aimed at helping the disabled, and the widows. Later with the adoption of generous service pensions, solidifying the party vote may have been important, although the numbers of beneficiaries were not that great. Finally, the motivation of patriotic fervor and gratitude for military service was also clearly important.

State and Local Efforts in the 19th Century

Whatever the reason for this allocation of governmental resources, we cannot conclude that this "northern soldier benefit program" was adopted to relieve the suffering of the poor. The United States federal government throughout the 19th century did not seriously address the problem of poverty. They left it, as the result of inaction, in the hands of local government, the churches, and other charities. There was a great deal of legislation by state governments in the last two decades of the 19th century, attempting to improve life in America, in education, housing, labor conditions, etc. For example, 31 states set up boards of health, 21 states adopted inspections of factories and workhouses for safety conditions, some states set up public employment offices, 24 states prohibited the employment of children under a certain age in factories (usually under 14 years). Many state laws were passed which were tangentially related to social welfare conditions. On the other hand, the United States national government did little (except for a law in the 1890s to reduce the hours of labor for women.) Contrary to the developments in West European countries during this period, there doesn't seem to have been even a serious debate in the United States Congress in the 19th century as to the national government's responsibility for dealing with the poverty in the land. State and local governments were the locale of any public actions to alleviate the misery of the poor. States did set up institutions dedicated to taking care of orphans, some of the elderly needy, juveniles, and special disabled citizens, such as the blind and the deaf. One survey revealed that 43 states had created benevolent and remedial institutions. This institutional approach to poverty was a continuation of what began already in the 17th century with the building of almshouses and poor houses in the colonial period.

The South–How was it Faring under Reconstruction?

What was happening to the poor in the South after the Civil War during Reconstruction? We have a considerable number of well-written histories of this period. Eric Foner's Reconstruction (1988) is an extremely detailed account. It was clear that social and economic conditions were appalling in the 1860s on to the end of the century in the South. As one Southern leader put it "the whole South is now bankrupt." The plantation owners were suffering although probably not as much as the freedmen and the poor whites. In the early Reconstruction period there seemed to be some hope that the former slaves and some whites working with the Republican political leaders would indeed institute reform. The blacks achieved considerable success politically, taking over major party state conventions and running successfully for state and local offices. There were 147 blacks elected to state legislatures, and nine were elected to the United States Congress. In some states like South Carolina they pushed through a platform agenda calling for debt relief, protection of the "poor man's homestead" and adopted a plank calling for governmental responsibility for "the aged, infirm, and helpless poor."[26] In Mississippi they pressed the army to set up a public works

program to help the poor of both races get jobs. In Georgia all debts dated
before 1865 were abrogated. The blacks strongly supported the "reformist,
activist state." But conflict was emerging with the conservative and wealthy
forces in the South. The new schools were crowded with blacks of all ages.
They saw evidence of considerable progress taking place. But it was short-
lived. Gradually the Republican whites took control of the states again.
With the election of Republican President Grant in 1872 reconstruction
continued, but Southern states were in desperate economic condition. And
the panic of 1873 did not help. Credit dropped dramatically and corruption
flourished in state capitals in the South. The result was a deepening depression and the destabilizing of Republican control in the southern states.
Every intent in legislation to help the poor pretty much disappeared under
these conditions. The Panic of 1873 of course, the greatest "depression"
ever, before the 1930s, affected the entire country. Banks closed, as did the
stock market, and many large and small firms were broke. There were labor
strikers and police repression, and the labor unions were demonized by the
press. Unemployment was high, as many as 25% in New York City, for example. There were so many unemployed men on the streets and roads and
"riding the rails" that vagrancy laws were passed, which led some states
to at least attempt to provide public works employment for some of these
men. The voters turned against the Republicans in the off-year election of
1874 and reversed a large Republican majority in Congress to a 60 seat
Democratic majority. Grant, however, was reelected in 1876 and in 1877
the troops were withdrawn from the South. The end of Reconstruction! A
major change occurred in the South. The whites acquired enough power to
rule without black support and the politics of oppression returned again.
"Reconstruction can only be judged a failure", Foner concludes.[27] By whatever yardstick, the protection of the citizen rights of the blacks, trying to
establish an "enduring Republican presence" in the South, or dealing with
the economic plight of the poor—these goals were really not met. There
were some efforts to help the poor in the South, even some small beginnings, but they did not last. And thus we had to wait long into the 20th
century before the plight of the blacks and the plight of the poor, white and
black, was significantly and forthrightly addressed in the United States.

The Poverty Crisis in the 19th Century: A Summary Evaluation

In assessing the historical patterns of the concern for, and care of the
poor, there is some evidence that a gradual change occurred after the Revolution. In the early 19th century poverty was certainly one of the most
critical problems facing American government and society. Some scholars
would say it was the most critical problem. The increase in population,
particularly in cities, accompanied by the increase in costs for communities seeking to care for the poor, the periodic panics and depressions with

their rise in unemployment, and the economic changes resulting from the industrial revolution—all of these resulted in a rethinking of the poverty problem and how to handle it. In 1824, for example, the secretary of state for New York put out a report based on data from all counties, revealing that $500,000 was being spent by government each year in New York to care for the poor. [28] There was great concern about poverty, about the types of behavior of some impoverished people, and the social consequences of this. Thomas Jefferson is quoted as writing "the mobs of great cities add just so much to the support of pure government, as sores do to the strength of the human body."[29] Protestant and Catholic churches were playing a major role in helping the poor, applying their evangelistic fervor to social problems. By 1820 some 1500 benevolent societies were started in New England, women particularly playing a major role in such benevolence. And special attention was paid to the indigent children. So there was a combination of private charity, religious activities and local/state governmental action. Moral reform became a major aim of such charity. But there was much controversy over who should be helped (the deserving poor) and what should be done to deal with the unworthy poor (the lazy, drunken, vagrants and beggars who lived on the fringe of society). Some cities had built huge almshouses, such as New York's Bellevue Home, built outside the city limits to isolate the paupers (so called) from the rest of the population. Baltimore built a similar almshouse isolating the poor who were put into this house. Philadelphia's costs had increased so much that in 1828 the city ended paying the costs of assistance to the poor. Thus the burden was greater and the question kept recurring—should we, and how should we, handle these problems. Seth Rockman suggests that a new consensus began to appear in attitudes, and strategies, a combination of three approaches: outdoor relief for the worthy, almshouses to be improved, and more discipline for the less worthy poor. Yet, there was never complete abandonment of public responsibility for the poor.[30] Poverty concerns remained central to the work of social reformers in the first half of the 19th century. But, as Rockman points out "the aspiration of private philanthropists and public officials departed from the optimism of the early republic."[31] Our big question is whether this change as noted had an impact subsequently on our approach to the problem of poor provision later in American history? One minority group which particularly illustrates the lack of national government interest in poor relief was the American Indian population. During the 19th and 20th centuries Indians suffered greatly as the result of wars, enforced resettlement on reservations, loss of land and of the basic means of decent survival. Whereas in 1800 it is estimated there were 600,000 Indians in the United States territory by 1900 they had been reduced to 250,000. Above all they became destitute. Reports were so alarming that in 1926 the

United States Government authorized a study of the living conditions of Indians. A study was done by the Brookings Institute under the direction of Lewis Meriam. This report in 1927 revealed the terrible conditions which the Indians had been subjected to. The report concluded as follows: "An overwhelming majority of the Indians were poor, even extremely poor, and they are not adjusted to the economic and social system of the dominant white civilization." In the areas of economic development, health services, and education, government programs were found to be terribly inadequate. We had driven the Indians out of their land and then had defaulted on our commitment to take care of them.[32] To sum up the American experience, we will pose seven questions, and on the basis of our research provide at best provisional answers:

1. Before 1900 did the United State national government reveal any interest or intention of taking responsibility for the poor? Not really, not specifically. There were some national figures who spoke about poverty but no one really for assuming responsibility. Civil War veterans were provided benefits but the major objective was other than inclusive poverty relief.

2. What was the character of the ideological rhetoric about poverty? The Puritan clergy did debate the question of caring for the poor, based on biblical interpretations. The defenders and opponents of capitalism also argued occasionally about it. But nationally there never was a basic dialogue among political leaders (for instance, in Congress). And there never was a debate at the national level among elites, as there was in Europe, over whether the national government should see poverty as a public function of the government (rather than a religious function) and at the national, rather than the local, level.

3. How did the local units of government in the 17th and 18th and 19th centuries deal with poverty? They did accept a considerable responsibility for the poor, passed tax legislation for poor relief, set up a system of overseers of the poor, and provided local institutions (almshouses and workhouses, etc.). As poverty increased, complaints about its cost increased, and there was some screening of the poor (especially by residential status). There seemed to be some minimal sense of collective effort and responsibility, but this was not consistent across time or across communities.

4. What role did the church play? The church never demanded that it was their sacred obligation (as was the case in some European countries). But the church did collect "poor chests" and make contri-

butions from time to time, particularly when local governments called on the churches for help.

5. What was the concept or characterization of poverty? There were from time to time attempts at distinguishing the "worthy" from the "unworthy" poor, particularly by the conservative clergy and the extreme proponents of capitalism. But generally in the colonies and later the poor were rarely denounced as "paupers" and never really as "criminals" (as we find in certain European systems.)

6. Among elites were there differences in their attitudes to the poor? We have only limited information on this. But one can deduce from what went on in the cities that political leaders certainly felt their responsibility to help the poor. And those local leaders with affluence, the merchants, who were also holding positions of authority in these cities, obviously must have been committed also to care for the poor. After all, these leaders had to initiate and adopt local ordinances financing the local poverty projects. On the other hand, national business leaders in the 19th century, or before, did not demonstrate any support for the public provision for the poor.

7. Finally, was there in America a consistent overtime approach to the poverty problem? Local governments did seem to persist in finding ways to help the poor, experimenting with different approaches and types of poor relief. But in reality no clear and coherent view of poverty relief and no clear and coherent solution to the poverty problem emerged—in a sense there was no cultural model established which could dictate the nature of a national approach to the poverty problem in the United States for the 20th century and beyond.

Notes

1. Gary B. Nash, *The Urban Crucible: The Northern Seaports and the Origin of the American Revolution*, (Cambrridge, MA: Harvard University Press, 1986), and Allan Kulikoff, *The Progress of Inequality in Revolutionary Boston*, William and Mary Quarterly, volume 28, no. 3, (July, 1971), 375–393, 400–411.

2. Kulikoff, *The Progress of Inequality*, 3.

3. Nash, *The Urban Crucible*, 11–12.

4. Nash, *The Urban Crucible*, 11.

5. Nash, *The Urban Crucible*, 115.

6. Kulikoff, *The Progress of Inequality*, 117.

7. Nash, *The The Urban Crucible*, 211.

8. Nash, *The The Urban Crucible*, 116.

9. Nash, *The The Urban Crucible*, 212.

10. Kulikoff, *The Progress of Inequality*, 3.

11. Kulikoff, *The Progress of Inequality*, 12.

12. Robert E. Cray, *Paupers and Poor Relief in New York City and its Rural Environs 1700–1830* (Philadelphia: Temple University Press, 1988).

13. Cray, *Paupers and Poor Relief*, 117

14. Cray, *Paupers and Poor Relief*, 102

15. See for example Michael P. Katz, ed., *The Underclass Debate: View from History* (Princeton, NJ: Princeton University Press, 1993).

16. Sidney Fine, *Laissez–Faire And The General–Welfare State* (Ann Arbor, MI: University of Michigan Press, 1978).

17. Quoted in Fine, *Laissez–Faire*, 187.

18. William G. Sumner, Essays II, 1911, 435, quoted in Fine, *Laissez–Faire*, 82-3.

19. This question from Gladdin is found in Fine, *Laissez–Faire*, 187.

20. See Fine, *Laissez–Faire*, 192.

21. Skocpol, *Social Policy in the United States: Future Possibilities in Historical Perspective*,(Princeton, NJ: Princeton University Press.) 37-71.

22. Skocpol, *Social Policy in the United States*, 45.

23. Skocpol, *Social Policy in the United States*, 37.

24. Skocpol, *Social Policy in the United States*, 55.

25. Skocpol, *Social Policy in the United States*, 55.

26. Eric Foner, *Reconstruction: America's Unfinished Revolution 1863-1877* (New York: Harper and Row, 1988), 305.

27. Foner, *Reconstruction*, 603.

28. Seth Rockman, *Welfare Reform in the Early Republic: a Brief History with Documents* (Boston: Bedford/St. Martin's, 2002), 168.

29. Rockman, *Welfare Reform in the Early Republic*, 7-8.

30. See Rockman, *Welfare Reform in the Early Republic*, for a discussion of this new consensus and its understandings, 18-24.

31. Rockman, *Welfare Reform in the Early Republic*, 27.

32. David Wallace Adams, *Education for Extinction: American Indians and the Boarding School Experience 1875-1928* (Lawrence, Kansas: University Press of Kansas, 1995), 331.

Chapter 8

A History of Poverty in Western Europe: The Dutch Experience

The insights from comparative history may reveal a variety of differential approaches to the resolution of the poverty problem. We continue this exploration by delving into the early history of the Netherlands. The key questions we focus on are: how extensive was the incidence of poverty in the early historical periods? What was the community response to poverty (i.e., what was the level and type of community responsibility), what actions were taken to provide for the poor, (and with what success), and how enduring were the policies and types of provisions for the poor—from generation to generation, and from century to century? Finally, and most important, how does the Dutch early historical experience with poverty compare with the American experience (as described earlier)?

Dutch history is a fascinating complex of many wars including six with England, several with France, and an 80 year war with Spain, as well as many conflicts among the cities and elites of the Dutch Provinces themselves. The condition of the "underclass" was fairly constantly one of considerable to extreme destitution. In the 15th century it is estimated that one-third of the population died of famine, the plague, and the wars. In the 16th century there was also religious persecution, particularly the killing of heretics by the Spanish Inquisition. Gradually through all this turmoil and conflict the seven key provinces of the Netherlands were brought together. There are reports that a Republic was actually proclaimed already in 1588, however this was not realized at that time. But it took over two hundred years more before the monarchy (the Kingdom of the Netherlands) was established, first by Napoleon in 1806 and then the monarchy of an independent nation under William I was proclaimed king of the Netherlands and Belgium in 1814. In the intervening years, particularly in the 17th century Holland had seen great affluence as a result of the success of the Dutch

East India Company leading to so much prosperity that this period was cel-
ebrated in Simon Schama's book, as "the Embarrassment of Riches." Yet,
as England took over with its dominance in sea power in the latter part
of the 17th century, the Dutch period of extraordinary prosperity gradually declined. However, even in this period of great prosperity (for some),
scholars wrote of the extreme poverty. As one writer put it "if one had to
choose an image that would characterize the society of this period, it would
be the beggar and the vagabond." To which was added the observation
"even during years of peace, the bulk of the population lived on the edge
of pauperism."[1] As we shall see the 18th and 19th centuries exhibited, at
least periodically, many years of considerable, often extreme, poverty.

Evidence on the Extent of Dutch Poverty

Historians have attempted to present data to document their conclusions on
the extensiveness and seriousness of poverty. They use different approaches
and measures. One fairly common one for those who study particular cities
is to determine from city registration and tax records what percentage of the
inhabitants earned enough to pay any taxes to the city. Those who were in
the lowest bracket (paid no taxes or less than five guilders) were considered
those in poverty. In the late Middle Ages and into the 16th century Jonathan
Israel found a high level of poverty from time to time. For example he
calculates in Leiden 33% poverty in 1514, dropping a bit later, but then
rising to 40% by the mid-1540s. [2] Sometimes the figures used are not
explained well and seem to be observations based on deep involvement with
the records of the period. Thus one scholar in his discussion of Amsterdam
states that in 1808 one third of the population of about 200,000 were on
"winter relief."[3] Another interesting case study, of Rotterdam in the period
of 1670 to 1700, does not hazard a specific percentage but presents evidence
of a high poverty rate: there were so many persons needing assistance in
Rotterdam at that time that the city magistrates had to adopt a policy
of refusing jobless immigrants the right to public charity. This, despite the
city's great variety of approaches to raise money to deal with the steady
increase in unemployment from the 1670s on.[4] Other studies of Dutch cities
(which calculated poverty on the basis of whether taxes could be paid),
revealed that in the 19th century Groningen had 70% poverty in 1890, and
Alkmaar 53%.[5] A sweeping conclusion of one major study of the 1815 to
1890 period was that a fourth of all households in the Netherlands were
in poverty, and that another 60% to 70% were living on the margins, with
no financial resources to keep them out of poverty if economic conditions
became worse. [6] In her book comparing France and the Netherlands in
the 19th century, Frances Gouda presents authoritative overtime data that
the number of Dutch people receiving poor relief increased to 500,000 by

mid century, and that total funding by public agencies (municipalities) and private agencies (churches and charitable organizations) reached 8 million guilders by that time, one fourth public and three-fourths private funding).[7]

The System and Culture of Dutch Poverty Over the Centuries

Scholars writing about poverty in the earlier period (16th and 17th centuries) report on the context and condition in which the poor lived which suggests special characteristics of the way in which people looked at poverty and responded to it. There was a feeling that poverty was a natural phenomenon in their community which they accepted as a social condition to be dealt with by the community naturally. In the early 15th century there was a "tangled mass of charitable foundations and endowments set up by individuals, guilds, and clergy." These were administered by different types of persons, frequently religious personnel. There were also monasteries of course dispensing relief. And "large" towns had their own hostels, orphanages, and sometimes small cottages for the poor. In the 16th century a "fundamental reorganization" of poor relief occurred, emanating in part from the Reformation, leading to new approaches to poverty. The medieval concept of poverty as a "sacred obligation" was not acceptable to the budding humanists. Thus begging, vagrancy, idleness, etc. were no longer acceptable. And aid for the poor was more centralized under the municipal boards. These changes took place in the south (Flanders and Walloon cities) and then moved north gradually until by 1570 (at the time of "the Revolt") when monasteries were closed and the cities developed centralized, public control of poor relief.[8]

There seemed to be few who passed moral judgment on the poor or looked critically at the destitute, blaming them for their own condition, labeling them as lazy, unwilling to work, preying on the rest of society, etc. There was some of this by a minority of the society. But the majority seemed to see that those living in unfortunate circumstances were persons whom the community must help. This was seen as a communal problem and hence a communal responsibility. One writer in trying to distinguish between the Dutch and the French attitudes to poverty claimed that the very terminology used to refer to the poor was unique and special in the Netherlands. The Dutch referred to the poor as the "behoeftigen" or the "needy", while the French used more frequently the term "paupers."[9]

From the 1590s on it appears that Dutch cities were adopting a new and better system of poor relief. In fact one scholar argues that what emerged was impressive, an "elaborate system of civic poor relief and charitable institutions so exceptional in European terms" that "there was probably never much likelihood in being emulated elsewhere." (A Venetian visitor in 1620 suggested it was financed by revenues taken from the Catholic Church). In the early 17th century Dutch cities were confronted with increased urban populations, unskilled workers, limited jobs, and increasing poverty. They had to act to deal with this. The key elements in their strategy were: (1) town governments took charge, and were autonomous, able to take over the institutions and funds of the Catholic church; (2) churches were tolerated for the distribution of poor relief, but under strict town hall control; (3) consistories (the governing boards of the Reformed Churches), could, and often did, play a major role in taking care of the poor. The motivations were diverse: economic conditions to deal with—at a time of short labor supply the poor and orphans could be put to work; there was also civic pride—a desire to do a good job of regulating what were called "the God houses"; recognition for prominent individuals who took part in setting up and contributing to, and managing the new system. (Those were "the Regents" whose paintings were commissioned by Amsterdam and other cities.) The poverty institutions, like the main hospital, were at the center of community life in a sense. Even the "mad houses" of Dutch cities were congratulated for being clean and "of good order."

The system was well organized, well administered, and as Israel puts it the product of "a quest for a well ordered, industrious care world based on confessional discipline." And of course in the last analysis it was a system aimed at proper social control.

Thus, by the beginning of the 17th century the civic welfare plan and system was fairly well established by cities, with some variations by cities, however. Poor relief was centrally organized, the object of certain tensions, even by "party-factional rivalries", but with the allocations and benefits distributed from a central fund under the control of the city leaders, or regents (the College of Almoners). The Reformed Church had a major influence. There were strict eligibility rules in cities like Leiden and Haarlem—denying aid to "outsiders", these with bad histories of behavior (such as gambling). Reformed Church membership was favored, and all the poor had to be registered.[10]

The church and special charities assumed a major responsibility for the care of the poor. Indeed, most of the leaders of the Dutch Reformed Church looked at poor relief as a religious obligation or duty. Schama has quite a bit to say about the role of the church in Amsterdam in the Golden Age of Dutch affluence. The church in effect told the wealthy Amsterdammers that they should use the money God had given them wisely, but they should at all times look out for the poor. Church members had to contribute regularly, and in many ways, with gifts to the poor in "Sunday boxes" passed around in the church, or by giving to those church members who came to their homes for contributions during the week, or by "tithing" for the poor, etc. The admonition was: "give, for one day you may be needy, as it pleaseth the Almighty." Passages from Scripture were constantly brought home to the rich—how difficult it is for a rich man to enter the kingdom of heaven, or how God had destroyed cities where the rich had been greedy, etc. Schama describes the church community as one in which the individual members were connected by a "chain of charity." This, in contrast to some Puritan ministers (in the American colonies) who used the Bible to argue that God expected people to work and "if you do not work, you should not eat." Most churches, in these early days took the major stance that the community had responsibility to care for the poor.[11]

Schama notes that visitors to Amsterdam during this period (17th century) commented on how well the poor were treated. This widespread provision for the poor and sick in the Netherlands was much admired by visitors even those who came from countries like England, where charitable institutions were well established. Embedded in early Dutch culture, then, was the emphasis on caring for the poor in a variety of ways. The church played an important role. But so did the municipal authorities. Indeed at times the community was subjected to much controversy over who should have primary responsibility. There were in fact three types of debates in Dutch history over who should have the responsibility for the poor. One was over the question as to whether the care of the poor should be a public function, rather than handled by private, charitable, or religious agencies. There was an interesting battle in the 1850s over what level of government should regulate local poor relief. The statesman Thorbecke claimed the state or public role and not a church role primarily (this is a battle he lost in Parliament). The second battle was whether the central government or local communities should assume responsibility. For most of this period, up to the 20th century, localities won out. And the third debate was over the question of the extent of the church's role. And the church won out except that the law assigned to municipal authorities the care of those poor who were not members of a church, or were not properly taken care of. The 1798 Dutch Constitution had actually described the poor as "the children of the state." And King William I had issued a decree in 1814 which urged national legislation, "to avoid that the needy will become victims of antagonistic opinions."[12] Yet in the end it was the local churches and local governments which took over the responsibility, until the 20th century.

In the 18th century following the Golden Age, there was a sharp economic decline in the Dutch provinces. People migrated from the towns to Amsterdam, or left Holland for other countries. Dutch ship building workers, for instance, left for other work abroad. Wages were low, jobs scarce, and the workers agitated with many strikes in Dutch cities. Labor organizations, were formed, and many guilds to support the jobless and the poor. The funds for the poor were set up, and programs to provide aid to the sick as well as accident insurance were created (the Catholics were often excluded from poor relief). The economic decline led to more poverty and greater inequality in income. For example, in one province (Overijssel) the poor increased from 25% in 1675 to 38%, while the nobility and rich burghers representing 2 to 3% of the population controlled 36% of taxable wealth in 1675 and 50% in 1758.[13]

A good overall description of the 1784–1854 periods by Van Loo discusses many aspects of poverty at that time. He reports that there was somewhat less poverty in rural areas than in the cities. There was much discussion among the people of what constituted poverty and when, under what conditions, it was manifest. Did it include more than inadequate housing, food, and clothing? Most people would identify the poor, and were ready and willing to help, in fact considered it a social duty. He reflects that poverty was perceived really as a "given", by most people and most poor. There was little evidence of a tendency to demean or degrade those in poverty. The church's role was primary in affecting people's attitudes about poverty. Many of the well-to-do wanted to, expected to, help the poor. A variety of approaches were used, including special institutions and poor houses (with careful instructions as to how to care for the poor). There were municipal administrators assigned the responsibility to work with and assist the poor: sometimes groups of citizens worked together in a sort of "cooperative" to raise money and distribute it to the poor. There was indeed concern over the increase of crime and its possible relation to the increase in poverty. Basically the image conveyed by this historian was that the community was aware of the considerable problems posed by poverty but was committed to care for the poor. It seems as if there was an ongoing socialization of the public in a city to think positively about the poor and to work together, whether through the church or outside the church, to support and provide for the poor.

Rotterdam
A Case Study of Poor Relief Administration About 1700

An illustration of how cities dealt with the administration of relief to the poor is provided by the excellent, detailed study of Carlson.[14] In the latter part of the 17th century as the Golden Age declined in affluence and glory, Dutch cities began to face economic decline, increased unemployment, the return of soldiers from the wars, and the beginning of migration to the city from rural areas. As the indigent migrants flocked to the cities, it became apparent that it was necessary to set up a system to deal with the homeless, hungry, and destitute, out of humanitarian considerations, legal obligations, and desire to forestall mass protests. Carlson suggests that Dutch cities used three types of systems: complete control by the churches in the distribution of benefits, control by the local magistrates who delegated responsibility to the churches and checked their performance, and assumption of primary control by the city magistrates who were at the head of a centralized community system of financing poor relief and administering it. Cities used variants of these three patterns.

In Rotterdam the pressure for action occurred early and resulted in experimentation with special systems of provisions for the poor. Already in the period from 1588 to the early 17th century the Reformed Church which was dominant, administered poor relief under the direct supervision of the city government. At that time there were two types of relief—at the home and in institutions (for the elderly, orphans, and paupers). These institutions apparently were already considered well run, with their own endowments and governing boards. Those who were unemployed and had no source of income were apparently well treated—receiving weekly allocations of bread, some money, blankets in winter, bed linen and some clothes. They also had access to subsidized medicine.

Reorganization became necessary because of changes in Rotterdam's population. By 1639 quite a few other religious denominations were active—the Remonstrants (an offshoot of the Reformed Church), the Lutherans, the Walloons, the Scots and English, and also the Catholics. The city council decided to turn care of the poor over to each church, to relieve the Reformed Church. The deacons of each denomination thus were given the responsibility for the administration of poor relief. To help reduce the number of eligible poor a two-year residence rule was put into effect. In 1649 so many Catholic poor had migrated to Rotterdam as a result of the Spanish War, the Catholics set up their own "poor chest" and began taking care of their poor. The Reformed Church's deacons were still left with the task of taking care of all non-church members, as well as their own poor. The city of Rotterdam was divided into districts (wijken) with a leader (wijken meester) in each district who monitored their areas to see that the proper people were assisted and the illegal immigrants (who did not meet residential rules) were not assisted. The church deacons, then, and these district masters were the persons who were intermediate between the population and the city magistrates.

The financing of this system was somewhat complex. There were Sunday collections for the poor, bequests from the well-to-do and legacies to the deacons, town subsidies, as well as local excise taxes, collection boxes placed all over the city, even a lottery (to collect funds for the poor) in 1695! Officials went door to door asking for contributions.

How should we evaluate this Rotterdam system? Obviously there was a strong and growing commitment to poor relief going back to the 16th century. A large part of the community was struggling with the questions of eligibility, administrative arrangement, financing. The church assumed, or was given, a major responsibility for poor relief. There seems to have evolved a culture and a system of taking care of most of the poor in the city (although we have no precise evidence on this from this case study). The elites in the city were not only involved, they were in charge. Their motivations are not completely clear, but they seemed to see the system as providing both social and political control. But as one reflects on such a study, one is inclined to feel that here were the beginnings of a truly societal approach to poor relief. Those involved in poor relief did it out of a mix of motivations—to help the unemployed, to feed the hungry, to minister to fellow "souls" in their own churches, and to maintain social control over the underclass. Rotterdam in 1700 is an enlightening example of all these motivations and functions.

As we move from the 18th to the 19th century a variety of developments relevant to the handling of poverty were occurring. A controversy was appearing about the role of the church and the state. The church saw the role of good Christians to be to take care of their poor church members, indeed the church was inspired to perform this role, and its members, particularly its rich members, by being generous (hopefully winning "heavenly interest" as a result.)[15] On the other hand government authorities were seeing poverty as their problem and their responsibility. There were demands to dismantle the religious and charitable institutions for the poor and have these taken over by the state. The early Republic in 1800 passed a Poor Law providing for better coordination of agencies (religious primarily) dealing with the poor problem. However, this law was considerably modified to limit state assistance only to those needy not cared for by the churches. But in 1815 the issue reappeared under King William I. Yet, despite the king's wishes the administration of poor relief remained in the hands of the locality, and the local church congregations specifically. However, the central government in the Hague sought to exert the "vigilance" mandated by the constitution over the nature of care for the poor at the local level. The king had issued a decree stating that the poor were "legally entitled" to assistance.[16] Yet, until the 1840s there were no real direct state efforts to intervene, despite the desire of national ministers and the king to do so. They were rebuffed by local authorities who wanted local control. In the 1850s, under the leadership of the Liberal leader Thorbecke the issue was raised again. The Dutch had adopted a new Constitution (1848) and a new municipal law (1851). The Constitution restated a national interest in the regulation of poor relief by law. Thorbecke argued that religious and private charitable organizations should be replaced by a "poor council that can be defined by law." And he introduced a new proposed poor law in 1854 to do this, that is, to assume state control over the administration of assistance to the poor for the entire country from The Hague. This was defeated in the Parliament, and thus care for the poor reverted again to the churches and the municipalities.

There had also been some conflict of views as to whether poor relief was proper under a capitalist system. To some scholars the free market system would not (could not) tolerate the allocation of large sums to the poor. Writers like de Bosch Kemper reasoned that "poor relief reduced mortality", and a society thus committed itself "to supporting a constantly growing number of people", and in the end there would be more poverty. Further, he argued, the large sums spent on poverty were a loss to the national economy. And the work performed by the poor in special poor houses did not compensate for this loss.[17] This attack on poverty as dysfunctional to free market capitalism was not, however, a major line of argument found in the writings of this period. There was during this period, and even earlier, much discussion of the English approach to poverty, particularly the Poor Law of 1834, viewed by some as one possible way to optimize the functioning of the market economy, and viewed by others as a gruesome experiment which put laborers in "colonies for the poor" to work under terrible, coercive conditions. The Dutch seemed to prefer their own, very different approach.

In fact in 1818 already a new approach to dealing with the poor was undertaken in the province of Drenthe. It was essentially a plan to set up "colonies" or farms for the poor, called the "weldadigheid" plan. It was quite successful and spread to other provinces, Overijsel and Friesland. It was seen at the provincial level, as a considerable success. It was continued until at least 1869.

A great deal of excellent scholarship was compiled by Dutch scholars on the state of poverty in the 19th century. Some very detailed data were available from them. Estimates of the number of poor suggest that the total number rose from 200,000 to 300,000 in the early part of the century to almost 500,000 by mid-century (out of a population of 2 million to 2.5 million). Expenditures by public and private (or church) benefactors increased from five million guilders in 1829, eight million by mid-century, and that number is estimated at almost 20 million guilders by 1900.[18] One scholar actually tallied the number of institutions for the poor which existed (for elderly, orphans, widows, unemployed, etc.). There were 5,298 in 1879 and 6,044 by 1897! The costs of taking care of the poor were distributed as follows: 30% by churches and private charities, 30% by individual contributions (small and large), 35% by municipalities, and only one to two percent by the national government in The Hague.[19] This suggests the expensiveness and continuity in allocations for poor relief, and the variety of sources for such funds. The Dutch really did take provision for the poor seriously.

It is important to note that all this was occurring really at the local level of the system, but under the vigilance of a very interested and concerned national government. The national elites were anxious to be involved, but the local elites were involved. Further, all this occurred before the rise of any major socialist movement in the Netherlands. It was the liberal and religious parties who were most deeply involved.

During the 19th century considerable social welfare legislation was adopted, by the national government, such as:[20]

1. Allowances were given (8 guilders) to every impoverished family which experienced the death of a child under the age of two (1860),

2. A ban on industrial employment of children under age 12 (1874),

3. Employment of women in factories limited to eleven hours a day (1889),

4. Factory Safety Act (1895),

5. Compulsory Education Act—at least six years in school (1900),

6. Neglected Children Act (1905).

A variety of social organizations were created in the 19th century pressing for such legislation. It was the Liberal party and Anti-Revolutionary party (linked to the Reformed Church) which were prominent early pushing this legislative agenda. Although the socialist movement was beginning there was no labor or socialist party until 1894. And they were not part of the Dutch government coalition until much later (1939). Thus, in five centuries of history, in which the Dutch public and Dutch leaders struggled to deal with poverty, the Dutch nation developed its own belief structure and institutions to deal with their poverty problem. As they entered the 20th century, they were ready for more action. The Poverty Law of 1912 was next!

A Summing Up

If we ask the same questions of Dutch history that we did for American poverty history, the answers are somewhat different.

1. Before 1900 did the national government express an interest in dealing with the poverty problem? Very much so, particularly after seven provinces became together the Republic and later Kingdom of the Netherlands. The early rulers and early constitutions recognized the problem and national leaders (like Thorbecke) argued strongly for national control in dealing with the problem. There was early commitment and a sense of public obligation.

2. The ideology of poverty, that is, how people thought about poverty and its amelioration, had a somewhat different content. There was a fairly benevolent feeling toward "the needy", even for some church members a "sacred duty" to help the poor. And society was responsible for the care of each individual. There were some concerns about types of the poor and certain requirements (e.g. residential) for aid. But basically there was a pervading sense of community responsibility.

3. Local governments took over much of the administration of poor relief. There were actually heated arguments as to whether the central government in The Hague or the municipalities should be in charge. The cities won this battle in the 19th century, much as they had performed it in earlier periods. And they experimented with a host of approaches beyond the levying of local taxes. But usually the local magistrates worked with the church wardens.

4. The church not only administered poor "outdoor relief" but helped build institutions for the poor. In addition the church kept reminding the well-to-do church members of their (biblical) duties to share their wealth (at least a part of it) with the poor.

5. In characterizing the poor, the Dutch rarely saw them as degraded "paupers" (as the French did) or as "criminals" (as some thought the English did), but as unfortunate members of society.

6. What was the attitude of the governing, social, and business elites? They were early active at the local level, organizing and financing the administration of relief, and searching for new ways to deal with the problem. At the national level they actually engaged in debates arguing for the assumption of governmental control over the handling of poverty. For the elites the issue was not whether the poor should be cared for, but by whom—the national government or the local governments in conjunction with the churches.

7. Was there historical continuity in the Dutch case? It seems that the answer is—very much so. While strategies for helping the poor changed over time, attitudes, beliefs, commitment, and a sense of social and government responsibility persisted, if anything becoming more humane and benevolent. Thus, an historical cultural path emerged, or a body of cultural orientations emerged, which may have influenced greatly the Dutch approach to such social reform in the 20th century.

Notes

1. C. Bruneel, in J.C.H. Blom and E. Lamberts eds., *History of the Low Countries* (New York: Berghahn Books, 1999), 232–233.

2. Jonathan I. Israel, *The Dutch Republic: Its Rise, Greatness, and Fall, 1477–1806* (Oxford: Oxford University Press, 1995), 123.

3. Frances Gouda, *Poverty and Political Culture: The Rhetoric of Social Welfare in the Netherlands and France, 1815–1854* (Lanham, MD: Rowman, & Littlefield, 1995), 72.

4. Marybeth Carlson, "Down and Out in Rotterdam in 1700: Aspects and Functions of Poor Relief in a Dutch Town" in *The Low Countries and the New World(s): Travel, Discovery, Early Relations*, Johanna C. Prins, Bettina Brandt, Timothy Stevens and Thomas F. Shannon eds. (Lanham, MD: University Press o f America, 2000), 40.

5. L.F. Van Loo, *Arm in Nederland 1815–1990* (Meppel, the Netherlands: Boon, 1992), 79.

6. Van Loo, *Arm in Nederland*, 174.

7. Gouda, *Poverty and Political Culture*, 78, 223–5. The original source was J. de Bosch Kemper, Geschiedkundig Onderzoek, (1951), Appendix.

8. Israel, *The Dutch Republic*, 123–124.

9. Gouda, *Poverty and Political Culture*, 38-39, This term "pauper" was considered more degrading. But this view was not necessarily supported by other students of French society. See Olwen Hufton, *The Poor of Eighteenth Century France* (Oxford: Clarendon Press, 1974), 17–18.

10. Israel, *The Dutch Republic*, 353–359.

11. See Simon Schama, *The Embarrassment of Riches: An Interpretation of Dutch Culture in the Golden Age* (New York, Knopf: 1987), 575-580.

12. Gouda, *Poverty and Political Culture*, 182, 184.

13. Israel, *The Dutch Republic*, 1012–1018.

14. Carlson, "Down and Out in Rotterdam."

15. Gouda, *Poverty and Political Culture*, 181.

16. Gouda, *Poverty and Political Culture*, 186.

17. Gouda, *Poverty and Political Culture*, 133.

18.   Gouda, *Poverty and Political Culture*, 78, 224–5; Van Loo, *Arm in Nederland*, 89.

19. Gouda, *Poverty and Political Culture*, 223.

20. Gerald Newton, *The Netherlands An Historical and Cultural Survey, 1795-1977* (Boulder, CO: Westview Press, 1978), 91–92.

Chapter 9

The Early French and Belgian History of Poverty to 1900

The more one delves into the historical background of poverty in Western Europe, the more one is aware of the early origins and persistence of concern for the poor. For France we can begin with the 17th century because it is then that we find much data, quantitative and qualitative, on poverty. One finds an "agonized correspondence between priests (curés) and bishops", as well as with others over the big question of what is to be done about this. These letters and the records of hospices, overseers of charity, police reports, the Commission of Burglary, as well as church edicts and government edicts, special publications, newspaper articles, provide a wealth of information from the mid 17th century into the 18th century about the extent of poverty, its causes, and proposals for dealing with the problem. "Who are the poor" was a frequent question, and another was "who is to take care of the poor?" It is interesting to note that a broad view was taken early as to the nature of poverty. As Condorcet stated early "Poverty is a malaise inherent in all of the great society" (*toute grande societé*).[1] It affects all human relationships, within the family, within the community, and within society.

There were great variations in the extent of poverty, depending on the particular period and the particular area of France. The "chilling descriptions" by local priests of the starving people in particular villages in the Massif in the latter part of the 17th century are inclined to be too easily accepted as manifestations of the general conditions of destitution elsewhere. The actual amount of poverty is a matter of some controversy, for one reason because the term *"pauvre"* and indigent are not easily distinguished. And because of the regional variations, at one point it is estimated that the population of certain areas such as Brittany, Western Normandy and the Massif were extremely destitute (as much as two-thirds), while in other areas such as Dijon, Montpelier, Toulouse and Rouen the percentage was much less. Hufton concludes his discussion of this by stating that in the 18th century up to 1789 the poor and indigent constituted one-third ("and speculatively, perhaps as much as a half") of the total population.[2]

Comparatively some scholars have argued that there was much more poverty in Holland than in France. They suggest a four to one ratio. The descriptions of poverty in France, however, and the reports of the incidence of poverty suggest that such a comparison is perhaps faulty. The explanation advanced is that the rural character of France, compared to Holland, made a difference, permitting people in France to survive better because of their cultivation of their own plots of land. Another possible factor was the practice of "migration" in France. Every spring the males in the countryside who could not support their families would go down in the valleys for the summer to harvest hay, pick grapes, and help with the olive harvest—thus earning an additional amount to tide them over the winter. It is estimated that at least 200,000 French men did migrate all over France each year in search of such work.[3] Whatever the calculations, it is quite clear that the economic conditions under which a large proportion of the French public lived in the period leading up to the Revolution was pitiable. Periodically people lived in conditions of starvation and deep despair. Beggars roamed the countryside, one half of whom were children, and perhaps 10% were old men and women. France is described often as the land of the "wandering poor."

What was done to deal with this poverty? There seemed to have been at least four types of approaches: (1) Alms giving by churches and ecclesiastical foundations; (2) village funds consisting of gifts, grants by the wealthy, benefactions from the dying and other special contributions; (3) the *"hôpital géneral"*, or the charitable institution established with grants from the wealthy and the church to provide a place for the deserving poor to subsist and even given some work to do in exchange for lodging and food; (4) *"bureaux de charité"*, which constituted a pool of alms and other funds voluntarily given to be used in various ways to help the poor. Of all these different approaches the one that seemed originally to be the most successful was the *"hôpital géneral"*. The idea for this originated in the mid 17th century by St. Vincent, the emphasis being on a shelter where the poor could find lodging, food and for those who were able, work. A Paris experiment in 1655 was successful, funds and furniture, etc. being given by the church, with further communal actions to build an extension as required. The aim was to get the beggars off the streets and the worthy poor a place to be housed temporarily and given work and training for work. The government encouraged this plan but most of the funds came from the church or private charity. The project went so well that a royal edict in 1662 urged all towns to adopt the same plan. The Jesuits carried this royal

message all over France, preaching sermons on the idea and helping towns
to set up their own structures. As late as 1800 many towns still had such
a facility. But early on problems had developed. Larger towns could afford
such a building, smaller towns could not. Further, it was assumed that the
work of the poor would bring in income to help support the project, but
this did not really develop. So, large towns sometimes did well, providing relief for a considerable number of poor (Rouen in 1777 was caring for
2005 people). But donations declined, leadership withdrew, and support for
the idea ended. Gradually the *"hôpital géneral"* was greatly restricted in
performance.

By 1724 the government felt it should act and issued an edict of that
year. The government assumed that a new direction was necessary, particularly based on the *"hôpital géneral"* which it wanted to make into workhouses which would be places of incarceration of beggars and loiterers. The
1724 act divided the poor into the able-bodied and the invalids. The latter if destitute could present themselves and they would be cared for. The
able-bodied poor had to try to find work in 14 days and if this failed they
could present themselves and would be put to work, to repay the costs of
lodging and food. They would also get a small "gratification" —presumably
money! The alternative for them was to find work or enter the army. This
legislation went into effect, but it soon failed in implementation because of
lack of funds. The workhouse concept didn't work out. Thus in the 18th
century during the period from 1724 to 1789 the government kept trying
to make the 1724 edict successful, but it failed. The government did allocate some funds for this project (1,800,000 livres) in the middle of the 18th
century.

These efforts reflect the conflict in France in the 18th century between
the advocates of the church's role in providing charity and the anti-clerical
view (of the Enlightenment) that charity was a public function. The government became critical, hostile, to the *"hôpital géneral"* set up by the church,
because that system had become ineffectual, but on the other hand was not
willing to put large sums of money in a program of provision for the poor.

The French monarchy did in fact directly provide a certain amount
of funding to help the poor from the 1740s on. This was of two types:
occasional outlays during periods of acute economic distress, poor harvests,
or epidemics; the second was for the development of the concept of the
"atelier de chareté" or workhouses for charity. The concept of the atelier
was really pushed by the central government. It was planned to construct
these workhouses as well as industrial schools (although apparently this
latter objective was not really implemented.) The national government was
to allocate most of the funds to the local administration (the "intendant")
who would make the decisions on how the money was to be spent. One

third of the funds would be raised locally. The basic character of the plan was a public works program, in which unskilled poor (women, children, and those with no special training) would work on presumably simple building tasks (such as terracing) while the skilled men would do the bigger tasks of digging and paving roads, etc. The difference in the atelier plan were that all these poor workers would be paid wages, (rather than in kind) and the central government would provide the funds.

This early example of a nationally conceived and funded public works project for the poor was advanced as a substitute for voluntary charity controlled by the church. What happened from the 1740s to the 1780s was not a result which was originally expected. Records indicate that the plan was not put into effect in at least 50% of France, due to local conditions where such work was not appropriate (in the Alps and high country, for example), and limited funds. The industrial schools were never realized apparently. So the evaluation by students of the project is that it was an experiment of limited success. Sometimes the central funds were not adequate, sometimes these funds were not properly handled at the local level, etc. But it did work in certain areas quite well. As one scholar reports, it was amazing what some of these poor women did in carrying heavy stones and tearing down ramparts of old cities, work for which they were ill prepared. But the overall impact of this experiment in dealing with poverty was very limited. The government did spend in the 1780s up to fifteen million livres. But this actually helped a very small number of the poor. One scholar concludes that these funds were actually "restricted to a very special section of the poor."

What was left for many of the poor was called "informal relief." The research on this is very interesting, reporting in a very touching way how the French people in many neighborhoods tried to help their poor. In certain neighborhoods begging took place by "previous agreement, even by appointment"! The local priests described these procedures. The neighbors knew who were the poor in their area and developed commitments and procedures for feeding them. Children knew which house to go to for breakfast (a slice of bread and later a cup of milk), and then mothers knew when and where they (the mother) could go for a bit of lunch (a slice of bread dipped perhaps in a sauce or a stew). The neighbors also shared their leftovers, the scrapings of the main meals. The poor households were also assigned to certain houses and the elderly were given special attention—regular callers brought scraps of food. Thus the parish fulfilled its charitable role which St. Vincent de Paul wanted. Of course this depended on a well-to-do set of neighbors or a wealthy "seigneur" or priest, and the willingness of people to help and donate. In certain parts of France there were too many poor and too few well-to-do for this type of relief to be common.

To sum up our findings about 17th and 18th century France is not simple. There was a great deal of poverty and indigence in France. In the 18th century it became worse. Sometimes the hard pressed poor would menace the well-to-do. Sometimes roving bands of wandering poor formed into gangs of ruffians and bandits who threatened villagers. The French government faced the problem by allowing the Catholic Church to bear most of the burden of caring for the poor, which the church did willingly as a holy act of charity. Later the government intervened to urge other solutions, sometimes with financial support sometimes without such support. What was unique in France was the special type of role of the Catholic Church, the early efforts of the monarchy to be involved (the edicts of 1662 and 1724, for example) and its major effort to restructure the system after 1740, with very limited success. The French poor often devised their own strategies, such as the yearly migrations of the males to the valley to harvest crops for wages and livelihood. Also perhaps unique was the informal, neighborhood patterns of helping the poor. These diverse approaches unfortunately left many to starve. The French, thus, tried a variety of approaches to care for the poor but in their early history they could not cope completely with their problem.

The major distinctive emphases in the French history of care for the poor up to 1789 are then as follows. There was an assumption by the church (or churches) of a major sense of responsibility for the poor. Second, there was a continual conflictual-cooperative relationship between the government and the church as to who should be primarily in charge. In France the central government played a role in seeking to define the strategy for the provision of care for the poor. Third, there was a broad vision of what the nature of poverty was, its causes, and its effects on human relations and the society. This was a philosophical, sociological, and moral set of perspectives. And, finally, one must remember that many of the affluent members of the community took a deep interest in helping care for the poor, partly at the urging of the church, partly as a motivation not necessarily linked to "salvation." Without the help of the wealthy care for the poor in the 17th and 18th centuries would have been much more meager and much less effective.

Changes in France in the Care for the Poor: The 1789 Revolution to 1900

The French Revolution quickly made a major change in the philosophy and practice of provision for the poor. In the roughly ten year period from 1789 under the Constituent Assembly a new poverty policy was announced which lasted roughly until the Directory period (1795–99), when it became clear that this new policy could not be afforded, and it was in a sense abrogated by Napoleon's decrees in 1800. The new Revolutionary policy stated bluntly that poor relief was the moral and political responsibility of the state, (not the church), indeed it was the "sacred duty" of the state. As one of the Revolution's spokesman, François Liancourt put it, "all human beings have a right to subsistence—if there are miserable people it means society is badly organized—society must provide sustenance to all of its members who are deprived of it and this helpful assistance must not be regarded as a gift—it is an inviolable and sacred debt society must pay."[4]

And so, the Constituent Assembly sought to take over the administration and costs of all poor relief. This included the work of the church in all communes and the 2,000 plus hospitals run by the Catholics to care for the poor. But it soon became obvious that this represented a huge task and a huge cost. And soon the policy was attacked as a very unwise one, "into which the exaggerated philanthropy of the Constituent Assembly pushed us." From 1795 on most officials saw the impossibility of implementing such a policy so suddenly adopted. And therefore by the 1800–1802 period under Napoleon the Catholic Church was allowed to reconstitute its charitable orders and institutions.

Yet, the central French state did not relinquish its control and supervision of the administration of poverty. This was the major change which was a residual of the Revolution and which continued throughout the 19th century. The state required the Catholic Church to secure permission from state authorities to set up hospitals, poorhouses, etc., and the state monitored the performance of churches as well as departments and communes in the administration of poor relief. The state also provided considerable funds.

Great philosophical and sociological and political debates occurred in Paris and elsewhere during the 19th century. There were those who recalled fondly the paternalistic dictation of the Assembly. At the other extreme there were those who reminded people of the criminal behavior of some of the poor, or the improper life styles of the beggars and vagrants. There were extreme advocates, by the police administration in Paris, for example, who argued for better laws to imprison beggars. There were those who saw poverty as "God's judgment" on the individual poor person, and those who argued that poverty was a function of systemic conditions, particularly the malfunctioning of industrial capitalism. Remembering the Revolutionary slogans of "liberty" and "equality" there were those who interpreted these as meaning that indeed all persons were born equal and with equal chances to succeed—thus no help was needed. And the role of the church, what it was and what it should be, in aiding the poor was debated. A social Catholicism emerged in the 1820s. They argued that the church was "the redemptress of poor people, the auxiliary to all just social reforms." But few Catholics wanted the church to have central authority and responsibility.

In all of these discussions, as Frances Gouda reminds us, there were four major issues or concerns (or objectives) that people, and the state should keep in mind. The first concern was over equalization. By helping the poor and disadvantaged you could improve their status in society, and narrow the social gaps. For some people this might be deemed socially advantageous. A second issue was the possibility that people would develop bad habits or motivations or behavior—lack of industriousness, unwillingness to learn skills, laziness, etc. Montesquieu indeed refers to this tendency in communities with good programs of caring for the poor. A third concern was over the possibilities that the poor would band together and engage in protest behavior, and that adequately providing for them could perform the function of pacification. Thus poor relief could prevent social disorder and political uprisings, a motivation which some have ascribed to Bismarck in Prussia in the 1880s. A fourth interest was the impact of poor relief on profitability of the economic system. This could be argued two ways: poor relief would provide more able-bodied workers and thus more economic products and more consumers; or, that the poor were only "outliers" and could only hamper the success of capitalism, unlikely to be productive workers and thus a burden on the system.

Another type of discussion concerned the evaluation of the English Poor Law of 1834. To the English was attributed the term "pauperism" equated with "popular misery" which to some French was a wrong way of characterizing the poor. Yet the word's origin in English was understandable to some French because "popular misery is greater in England than anywhere else." This was particularly related to evaluations of the English Poor Law as a gruesome way to deal with the poor, institutionalizing them under horrible conditions rather than giving them outdoor relief. And, of course, the rationale for the adoption of the Poor Law as necessary for a productive capitalist system, was somewhat related to this rejection of the English approach and terminology.

Despite all this debate and highly conflicted ideology about poverty, the reality in France was that control was centralized, Paris was the center where the decisions were in fact made, under which the Catholic Church in its administration of poor relief, worked. And one should note that the French government allocated financial support generally, as well as in special times of crisis, to poor relief. The accompanying table (9.1) tries to present over time data on this. These data provide some evidence of the extent of the national government's involvement in poor relief. By all evaluations of this effort it seems clear that it was not by itself adequate at all. Local efforts of the church and private charity carried a major load.

France continued to wrestle with its poverty problem during the 19th century. Industrial capitalism, however, complicated the picture, particu-

Table 9.1: French Data on Support for the Poor in the 19th Century

A. Budget Allocations for Public Workers

Year	1816	1817	1844	1846	1850
francs (millions)	9	21	149	201	149

B. Budget Allocations for Charitable Institutions

Year	1856	1937	1844	1846	1847	1848	1849
francs (thousand)	643	1,116	439	1,115	5,303	1,683	904

C. Expenditures on Outdoor Relief

Year	1833	1841	1847	1849	1851
francs (millions)	90	140	200	150	160

D. People Institutionalized for Poor Relief

Year	1833	1841	1849	1851
People (thousand)	500	600	670	600

Source: *Statistique de la France:* Administration publique, 1861, pp. xxix; statistique de l'assistance publique, 1861, p. ixvii, reported in Gouda, 1995, 207, 208, 209, 213.

larly producing much discussion of the conditions under which the working class was living and working. But no major social welfare legislation was adopted, until 1895 when the first French Poor Law was passed. Yet, it took a long time before the state returned to consider the basic ultimatum of the Revolution again, particularly its 1790 dictum that the state had a public obligation to care for all the poor.

Our concluding observations on France, using the set of seven questions posed earlier, would be as follows. France's experience with poverty differed significantly from both that of the United States and the Netherlands. First, the national government did not seek a major role until the Revolution of 1789. Under the monarchy there was some interest and royal edicts proposing more local assistance. In 1789 the government proclaimed that caring for the poor was the responsibility of the central government, the Revolutionary leaders asserting and assuming the moral and political responsibility for the poor. Subsequently, the actual care for the poor was devolved on the Catholic Church but under national supervision.

Second, ideologically poverty was conceptualized in a variety of ways.

Despite the Revolutionary doctrine of benevolence toward the poor there was periodically a deep-felt negative reaction to poverty. The poor were seen as the lowly "paupers" , and many were considered unworthy of help. The Paris police chief in fact asked Parliament for power to put the criminal element among the poor in prison. However, the church's attitude was very humane.

The local units of government assumed a great part of the responsibility for dealing with the poor, sometimes in cooperation with the church and at other times in conflict with the church's approach to charity. Thus in the early 18th century (1740 on) the government adopted a public works program (the workhouses) while the church was operating its voluntary charity program. The Catholic Church clearly played a major, vital role in caring for the poor, despite its conflicts with the central and even local governmental leaders.

The role of political and wealthy elites in the provision of poor relief varied from period to period and was influenced by elite attitudes toward the poor. There are considerable signs that the affluent in French society in the century leading up to the Revolution were contributing with gifts and large sums for establishing charitable institutions. In the "informal" neighborhood relief the rich also contributed on a regular basis. And later they were influential in providing funds for the workhouses and almshouses of the 19th century. Thus, it is clear that elites in government and out of government were involved. The government edict of 1724 was an early example.

Finally, was there a basic pattern of poor relief over time which one could say clearly defined the French approach to poverty? This is not clearly evident. There were a variety of attempts and experiments which were more or less successful. But no persistent ideology or administrative approach emerged. While there was a strong commitment to help the poor no definitive "French poverty culture" developed by 1900 which would predict what the French would do in the 20th century. The Dutch pattern seemed fairly well set, and different than the French. The United States had not demonstrated any clear, articulated approach at all. These systems, thus, were highly differentiated, historically, in their approaches to poverty.

Belgium: A Brief History of Poverty in the Early Years

Belgium received its independence in 1830. Before that it was ruled from time to time by different European powers. It consisted of the southern provinces of the low countries, an area not a part of the Dutch Republic proclaimed in 1588, which included only the seven northern provinces of the Netherlands. In the early 18th century (1713) it was taken over by the Austrian Emperor Charles and Empress Maria Theresa, and remained under

Austrian control, with occasional disruptions, until 1790 when the independent Batavian Republic was created. That did not last long, however. The French occupation followed, with Napoleon in 1806 declaring his brother king of the Southern Netherlands. With Napoleon's defeat in 1815, these "Belgium" provinces reverted temporarily to the Austrians, who lost them in a revolt in 1815, at which time it was included in the Northern Netherlands (now a monarchy under King William I). But the southern provinces revolted again and in 1830 received their permanent independence, also a monarchy under King Leopold.

The extent and conditions of poverty seem, according to historical accounts, to have been similar to those described in our discussion of the Netherlands earlier. From the 17th century, and even earlier, there are reports of considerable privation. As one study puts it for this early period, "the bulk of the population lived on the edge of pauperism."[5] At that time there were charitable institutions which attempted to deal with poverty, but it was not well coordinated. There was considerable concern, but no systematic plan and, thus, the care of the poor was left in the hands of the Catholic Church. Charles V respected local authorities in their roles, apparently without any real supervision. At times the amount of poverty was considerable, when special conditions existed—as in the grain crisis of the 1690s, the famine of 1693, and the hard winters in the early 1700s. The poverty was then characterized as "gigantic."

One of the early reactions was to stigmatize the poor as vagrants and beggars, and these were so numerous that laws were passed to imprison them or to put them in "houses of correction", in the hope of teaching them how to work. Periodically throughout the 18th century, including during the term of Empress Maria Theresa, "beggary" was condemned, attempts were made to drive the beggars out of the city (or to keep them from entering) and to punish them sometimes in cruel ways. The poor seemed to roam from place to place seeking help.

It is interesting that in these early days those in authority were worried about the consequences of poverty. In 1750 a study was made in Brussels, using city records, to discover comparative evidence on the mortality of children born to the poor, compared to those born to the well-to-do and the nobility. They reported that out of every 1,000 births in poor families only 393 survived to age 10 while the figure was 726 for the wealthy and nobility.[6] Yet there is no evidence that these shocking findings led to any real efforts to care better for the poor.

There was apparently much discussion among the leaders in these cities and provinces about how to handle the problem. And from time to time certain remedies were attempted. Thus, Empress Maria Theresa had the idea that farms should be provided for the poor, and although a start was made, there was no systematic follow-up. There were arguments as to whether poverty should be treated as a crime or as a condition over which the individual had no control, a condition which was the result of economic crises or natural disasters. A book appeared in 1764, *Of Crimes and Punishments*, by Beccaria, which recommended that torture in judicial proceedings be abolished, which stirred quite a debate. This writer and others urged that "loafers" be treated more humanely.[7] This led to a new reformatory being built in Flanders (Ghent). Others followed with similar efforts. But the decentralized nature of the regime resulted in no systematic country-wide approach. Emperor Joseph, the son of Maria Theresa, tried to centralize charity at one point but this proposal was defeated, and local charity and local Catholic churches assumed responsibility and control. But the result of the discussion generated by the writers was that a distinction began to be made between "crime" and "poverty."

One finds evidence, somewhat surprising, of early 18th century study of poverty. In 1846 a study was made of the wages of industrial workers, which everyone suspected were not "livable." The study defined the "poverty line" (below which it was necessary to provide a worker a decent standard of living). This was set at 743 francs a year for a cotton worker. Then it was discovered that the average wage was well below that—656 francs a year. Other systematic studies in 1853 and 1854 found that only the best paid workers, (miners, and metal workers) were better off in wages than convicts in Belgium.[8]

It is clear that in Belgium in the 17th, 18th and 19th centuries there was a great deal of poverty, genuine concern about how to deal with it, a disorganized approach at the central government level, and a reliance on the church and private charity at the local level to deal with it. The approach was not always humane, the acceptance of responsibility not always clear. In these respects perhaps Belgium differed from the Netherlands. Unfortunately we do not have as many detailed, local studies in those early days as we had for the Netherlands. Also, the dominant role of the Catholic Church was different than in the Netherlands.

In the latter part of the 19th century Belgium began to develop its social welfare policies. As in the Netherlands these were minimal approaches. In 1889 the first law was passed regulating the number of hours which women and children could work; also, the provision of cheap housing for laborers. In 1903 accident insurance legislation was adopted, in 1911, pension insurance for mine workers.[9] These early policy actions occurred when the conservative (Catholic) party was in power. The Belgium Socialist Party was established in 1879 and the Belgium Workers Party in 1885. But neither of them played a role in early social welfare policy decisions, although they were beginning to agitate for such reform.

Notes

1. A major reference and a basis for this review is Olwen H. Hufton, *The Poor of Eighteenth Century France 1750–1789* (Oxford: Clarendon Press, 1974).

2. Hufton, *The Poor of Eighteenth Century France*, 24.

3. Hufton, *The Poor of Eighteenth Century France*, 72.

4. Gouda, *Poverty and Political Culture: The Rhetoric of Social Welfare in the Netherlands and France, 1815–1854* (Lanham, MO: Roman & Littlefield, 1995), 174–5.

5. J.C.H. Blom and Emiel Lamberts eds., *History of the Low Countries* (New York: Berghahn Books, 1999), 133.

6. Blom and Lamberts, *History of the Low Countries*, 156.

7. Blom and Lamberts, *History of the Low Countries*, 162–3.

8. Blom and Lamberts, *History of the Low Countries*, 321.

9. See Herman Deleeck, *De Architectuur Van de Welvaartsstaat Opnieuw Bekeken* (Leuven, Belgium: Acco, 2001), 42.

Chapter 10

The English Historical Experience with Poverty

The description and evaluation of how the English suffered with poverty and sought to deal with it is a long and fascinating study. The story is replete with very special acts considered progressive at the time, as well as various actions criticized and denounced. It is important history, however, necessary to understand alongside Dutch, French, German, Belgian and, above all, American history. In what ways was it unique, and in what ways similar?[1]

English historians take us back to the feudal period when the worker was a serf laboring for his lord. Theoretically he was taken care of, but he was very poor. And at the time of bad harvest he, as well as his lord perhaps, starved. But the status of the poor serf in these days was honored by the church, we are told, for he was told by the priest that he was "blessed" and was certain of salvation. Thus poverty when it occurred was actually a "blessed" condition.

The feudal period began to come to an end by the middle of the 14th century. This was due to the opportunities for a better life in the towns, working for woolen manufacturers and others. At first the authorities sought to keep the serfs from traveling and required them to continue to work as before. But before long the attitudes of the government were more liberal toward the poor. This punitive and repressive approach was replaced in the 1500s by an acceptance of the needs of the poor and the need for poor relief. Begging in the 16th century became an acceptable form of self help. In addition, three other types of poor relief appeared—benefits from merchant guilds, bequests by charitable foundations (460 existed in England by the time of the Reformation), and finally the assumption of poor relief by the church linked to its conception of helping the poor as its sacred duty and role. Above all the government accepted its role under Henry VIII. In 1531 his statute was the first time the government of England took positive responsibility for relief of economic distress. Supplemented by later laws such as that of 1536 the King sought to set up a system of charity to be administered by the "mayors, justices of the peace, and other local officials." Certain types of begging were legalized. And a system was set up for the collection of funds to be used for poor relief.

In 1601 the Elizabethan "poor law" was adopted based on these experiences from Henry VIII on. This law firmly established the "parish system" for dealing with poverty which lasted into the 19th century. It became the responsibility of the parish to take care of the poor within its boundaries. The parishes were empowered to levy taxes to meet the costs of relief. And as these taxes increased there developed over the years criticism of the extent of help to the poor, and pressure to modify the system. The parishes provided relief in different ways; through "outdoor relief", building of workhouses where the able bodied poor could be put to work. In 1722 a law was passed facilitating the building of more workhouses. Eventually the poor were virtually forced into workhouses by parish officials, if they sought poor relief. The aim was to gain economically by putting poor families to work under supervision and in a residential setting. The poor loathed these workhouses because of their inhumane living conditions.

During the latter part of the 16th and the entire 17th and 18th centuries, the ideology driving the operation of the poor law was increasingly repressive. A distinction was made between worthy and unworthy poor. This ideology was abetted by the Calvinist Protestant ethic concerning work: working hard was God's will and the lack (or refusal) of work for the able bodied was a sin, contrary to God's will. Further, in a time of economic prosperity it was claimed there was employment for everyone who genuinely wanted it. Thus, poor people were no doubt lazy if they were unemployed, and it would be necessary to coerce them to work. Further, the ruling elites were well-to-do and their relationships to the poor lower class began to change. In feudal times the ruling class had a sense of moral obligation to care for the poor. But with the advent of industrial capitalism doctrines of self-help, individualism, and laissez-faire dominated elite ideology. The treatment of the poor by the landed aristocracy in England, a fairly rigidly stratified system, led to the special form of British liberalism (not a revolution as in France!). The individual (poor as well as wealthy) should rely on his own skills, utilize his own opportunities, and accept his own fate.

Under the Elizabethan code there was a gradual and progressive deterioration of the status of the poor person in English society. The unemployed were at the mercy of the parish officials. Those who ran the poor relief system in each parish could use a variety of approaches. They could put unemployed in the houses of parishioners as sort of indentured servants, forced to work for their keep. They could refuse to give relief to the undeserving. They ran the workhouses as they saw fit and they began to develop and use the principle of "limited eligibility", that is, no person on poor relief should be given more money than that of the lowest paid worker in the area.

The number of workhouses increased. By 1800 about one fifth of all paupers on permanent relief were in workhouses—most communities of market size had workhouses. There were about 3,765 by 1803. A large percentage of those on poor relief were not in workhouses (estimated at two-thirds), but the pressure was mounting to decrease this "outdoor relief."

A variety of factors led to the adoption of another Poor Law in 1834. The costs of poor relief had risen sharply—in 1832 it was 5 times what it cost in 1760. The tax burden was on householders and property owners (not on manufacturers). There was some argument that fewer people were working and the quality of work was poor. Dissatisfaction with the administration of the law was high. The argument was that the poor were "improvident." Public leaders argued to decrease the funds for "outdoor relief", to implement fully the rule of "limited eligibility", and to rely more on the workhouses for helping the poor. A Royal Commission of Inquiry was appointed in 1832. The report of this commission was very negative in its evaluation of the parish system. It recommended use of the workhouse much more for poor relief. The new 1834 Poor Law did exactly that, established the workhouse as the major instrument for providing poor relief. As one observer of the day commented, the aim of this law was "to devise means for rendering relief itself so irksome and disagreeable that none would consent to receive it." Others condemned the new law as extremely punitive. The political leader Disraeli stated soon after the new law's adoption: "It announces to the world that in England poverty is a crime."[2]

The 1834 Poor Law was particularly significant because it was a product of central government action aimed at central government control and administration of poor relief through local agencies. A Poor Law Board was appointed. The law set up what some called a "harsh" set of regulations, or a "moral code." The ruling class revealed its prejudices in dealing with the problem of providing for the poor. Hard-nosed "deterrent" workhouse relief was what they insisted on. One might add that this included exploitation of children at low wages, long hours of work, under unhealthy conditions. In the long run this very questionable piece of legislation led eventually to very repressive social reform.

For most of the 19th century after 1834 there was continual and in fact increasing debate over the principle and apparatus of the Poor Law Board. The newspapers opened their pages to public comment. Special articles were written by those on both sides of the issue. Gradually a growing consensus developed that the approach England had taken under the 1834 Act was too harsh and inhumane. The descriptions of the conditions in these workhouses were alarming, from Charles Dickens' *David Copperfield* (1837) to Disraeli, Lloyd George, and many other notables. Indeed it is significant that it was the intellectuals, the liberal clergy, politicians, and well-to-do businessmen and women who played a major role in evaluating and condemning the workhouse system as it functioned from 1834 on. Many of them banded together to create in 1869 a major new philanthropic organization called the Society for Organizing Charitable Relief. Through their organization there was a system set up for centralizing the personal and group charities into an organization to which those needing relief could apply directly. It was designed to help the many poor who would not enter the workhouses.

Several major studies were undertaken to get at the facts of poverty. One of the most famous was that of Charles Booth a business man who decided to do a complete study of poverty in London. He wrote a 17 volume study based on his, and his group's, research studying and interviewing the poor in London. It was published in the 1880s as *The Life and Labour of the People in London*. Charles Booth worked for 17 years on this project while also being a top official in the Booth Steamship Company. His was an empirical study of, as he put it, the poor "as they actually exist." He concluded that over 30% of the London population lived in poverty.

This attack on the 1834 system for dealing with the poverty problem finally came to a head when Parliament appointed in 1905 a Royal Commission on the Poor Laws and Relief of Distress. The Commission included representation of those running the current Poor Law administration, who were a majority, and representatives of the opposition including the Fabian socialists and the unions. The four persons in the opposition included Beatrice Webb who with her husband Sydney played a leading role in changing the system. After much testimony (159 hearings and 452 witnesses) and arguments by outstanding leaders on both sides, a decision was reached. It was agreed to call the new plan "the Public Assistance Act" instead of the "Poor Law Act." The workhouse approach was to be abandoned as unsuitable for the able-bodied poor. The focus was to be on "treatment" not on punishment, on helping the poor rather than "deterrence." Outdoor relief was to be revived. The Commission's report expressed the hope of having "a more constructive policy" in dealing with the poor. Thus, the 1909 Royal Commission set the stage for a whole new era of reform, based on new principles. The report recommended a national system of employment exchanges, a better child labor law, more technical education, and the planning of public work to help during periods of economic crisis. As for the regulation of poverty, a new regime was to be set up under a "Registrar of Public Assistance" who would supervise the provision of relief through the various governmental agencies. Thus in 1909 England entered the 20th century with a new and more generous, more humane, approach to social reform and care for the poor.

In concluding this brief review of English history, it may be useful to summarize the key aspects of the English engagement with poverty. It is quite clear that the English went through a long period from the 16th century on of searching for a way to help their poor, of which there were many. The government and its citizens went through long periods of struggling to find a satisfactory strategy. From 1601 to 1909 there were laws, actions, policies which were very harsh and ungenerous, even brutal. And this led to relief programs which were often disastrous. In the early centuries perhaps the English authorities were more kind, understanding and helpful than in the later years.

If we ask of the English history the same questions we put to the Dutch, the French, and the Americans, we find some similar, some different observations. One must realize that the problem was always with the English, and one must admit that the English constantly sought a satisfactory approach. And the national government was certainly engaged in the effort to find an answer—from Henry VIII in the sixteenth century, to Queen Elizabeth in the early 17th century, to the long period leading to 1834 and finally to the 1905 Royal Commission. The national government was involved, admittedly often times negatively. Local authorities and the churches and private societies and charities were also involved.

The conception of poor people as paupers (like the French), and indolent, parasitic, exploiters of public aid was often the case—and this interfered with a healthy constructive approach. Nevertheless there was a real sense of responsibility to take some action, to provide some relief. But this did not necessarily result in good policy. Perhaps the 1834 Act is the best example of that. Above all, however, what English history reveals is great change in concept, in strategy, and in policy, in the ability to reverse biases and poor strategies. One must remember that by 1908 to 1911 the English adopted their first versions of an old age pension law (1908), a national health insurance law (1910, 1911), and their early unemployment compensation act (1911). Later, in the 20th century the English experience led to the adoption of a very modern, humane social reform policy, which we will analyze along with our other countries in a subsequent section of this study.

Notes

1. Of the many studies of the English history of poverty we have relied most heavily on the following: Karl de Schweinitz, *England's Road to Social Security: From the Statute of Laborers in 1349 to the Beveridge Report of 1942* (New York: A.S. Barnes, 1973); Victor George, *Social Security and Society* (London: Routledge and Kegen Paul, 1973); M.A. Crowther, *The Workhouse System, 1834–1929: The history of an English Social Institution* (London: Batsford Academic and Educational, 1981); Gertrude Himmelfarb, *Poverty and Compassion: The Moral Imagination of the Late Victorians* (New York: Alfred Knopf, 1991).

2. De Schweinatz, *England's Road to Social Security*, 124.

Chapter 11

Sweden and Germany's Historical Experience with Poverty

The early history of Sweden is intertwined with that of other northern European countries such as Denmark, Norway, and Finland. In fact, histories lump them together, referring to these as "Norden" or "Scandinavia." Yet, for most of history one can separate out Sweden for special attention. It is difficult to describe poverty in a specific and precise way because Swedish historians do not (in English at least) deal with it the way American, Dutch, French, and English historians discuss their historical treatment of poverty. Nonetheless, one can construct a description based on our knowledge of the nature of the society, particularly at the lower, underclass, level of the Swedish society.[1]

If one goes as far back as the 16th century, or even the 15th century, historians describe the life of the Swedish people in a special way. There were only 900,000 to a million persons in Sweden then, and their living conditions were referred to as "harsh", with the serfs scratching out a living from small land holdings or as laborers for other land holders. Most of the 90% of the population who lived in the rural areas were struggling to survive under subsistence farming. And people developed a collective spirit of neighborhood assistance and communal sharing, and cooperation.

From 1500 on changes took place gradually, economically, socially, politically, religiously, but the basic character of human relations seemed to be well established. At the top were the nobles (about 1 % of the population) and the friends of whoever was the monarch at a particular time. And the rest were the rural proletariat. Even in 1800 80% of the population lived an agrarian existence.

The status, or fate of the rural poor, was exacerbated by the control and exploitation of the land by the nobility. The nobles acquired land as gifts from the Crown, with no requirement to pay taxes, and in turn taxed the peasants as heavily as they could. This practice delayed the development of the middle class, and left the peasants at the mercy of the nobles and the uncertainties of the harvest each year. Eventually, in the 19th century peasant revolts occurred and the kings were forced to take back much of the land they had given to the nobles.

Much of Sweden's history is told by reference to the frequent succession of monarchs and the many wars they fought in. In the 16th century alone there were eight monarchical succession episodes; in the 17th five different kings. In the 17th century alone Sweden was at war for 52 years. This included the thirty year war from 1618 to 1648. They fought Denmark several times, Russia also more than once, as well as the Habsburgs and the Holy Roman Empire, including, German states, Poland, and others. They were also engaged with, or against the French and the Dutch. The irony is that after all this fighting Sweden had lost Denmark, Finland, (and other possessions) and had not achieved the Baltic supremacy which it had hoped for. Above all, the costs of these wars were great—kings died in battle, and thousands of soldiers perished (16,000 were captured and taken off to Russia as the result of one engagement alone). Who paid the price of war? The peasants mostly, as higher taxes were levied and extracted from them. There were other developments of course, such as the introduction of Lutheranism in the 16th century, which became the state church eventually. Education was promoted by some of the kings, and universities like Uppsala and Lund developed distinctiveness, with able scientists. The influence of the Dutch and French was also beginning. Sweden also attempted its own imperialism, founding "New Sweden" in America (on the Delaware River) in 1638, but then lost this colony to the Dutch in 1655. A trend toward the development of town as well as commercial enterprises began, but those efforts were relatively minor until a century or so later. Yet, a trend did occur in the appearance of a so-called "middle class" of merchant entrepreneurs. But the 17th century was in reality one of contrasts, characterized by one scholar as: "contrasts of new affluence and continued poverty, boom and bust, innovation and tradition." [2] Basically it was a time of conflicts between king and nobles, of increasing cost of government, and "the triumph of absolutism." At the end of the century some of the commoners were far worse off than before.

The 18th century was supposed to be the "Age of Enlightenment", but also as the "Age of Revolution." Enlightenment implied more political freedom, limited monarchical authority, more reason and humaneness in society and its governance. Yet, this was hardly the case in Sweden. The century began under absolutism and ended under Gustav II Adolph with still a fairly absolutist constitution. In between, from 1719 to 1772 there was an interlude of semi-parliamentary and limited monarchical government. But the reforms which were adopted referred primarily to the role the nobility would have in the system. There was a new type of conflict, between two parties called the "Hats" and the "Caps", but it collapsed in the end. Above all, the political system was organized from the top down, and the peasants played essentially no role in it. Nor was the life of the peasants, their status, opportunities, and assistance noticeably altered during this period. There were four estates in Sweden: the nobility, the clergy, the burghers, and the farmers. The farmers' lot was not really relevant to the political changes. The peasants, still 80% of the population in 1800, were still the vulnerable underclass. As one scholar put it, in Sweden there was "no mass movement for revolution, no mob, no Bastille, no march on Versailles."[3]

The 19th century dawned in Sweden, and it was still plagued with absolutism. Democracy took a long time coming. The new 1809 constitution still was conservative although some limits on the king's power were imposed. In 1863 King Karl XV was forced into certain changes. The four estate Parliament was finally reduced to two estates and two houses, although the first chamber was dominated yet by conservative members. The nobility voted itself from the center of the political stage. But this was not yet a democratic breakthrough, and it took many years before the suffrage was opened up and proportional representation was adopted (in 1909). In the meantime throughout the 19th century the kings continued to engage in a variety of wars. The condition of the lowest estate, the farmers, did not improve appreciably. And by mid-century still 75% of the Swedish population was struggling for a sustenance by farming. Although historians do not give us much detail apparently the unrest was widespread among peasants (and others also). This resulted in 25% of the Swedish population (of about 5 million) emigrating to the United States or Canada during this period. It appears that there were several causes for this, including economic hardship. But opposition to the Lutheran Church, perceived as too hierarchical and too rigid in ritual and discipline, also played a major role. The period from 1870 on was significant because of the emergence of the industrial revolution. Rural life was no longer satisfactory or profitable for many, but they were not necessarily satisfied either with the types of jobs they found in the cities.[4] They were pressed to emigrate by the desire for better jobs, more land, more democracy, more open societies, and the chance to start over. While it is true that economic changes were taking place in Sweden during the 19th century, it apparently was not enough, or not apparent enough to hold these Swedish peasants to their homeland.

In the discussion of the history of poverty, Sweden is somewhat of an anomaly. Many writers imply it existed, sometimes disastrously. In the latter part of the 18th century and in the 19th century we finally get some estimates, as follows[5]

Year	Rural Poor	Total Population
1775	550,000	2,020,000
1800	730,000	2,387,000
1870	1,278,000	4,169,000

Presumably in the earlier periods, and to the mid 19th century the Crown aided his subjects, and the rural poor helped each other. In the 1840s and 1860s the Swedish government began to seriously discuss the need for more governmentally provided poor relief. The liberalist philosophy which dominated governmental circles raised serious questions as to the advisability of dealing with the poor through national legislation. Much of the debate was negative, particularly in the 1860s at the time of great famine. The classic liberal arguments were advanced–that the poor had only themselves to blame, and that private charity should properly deal with the problem, that it was not a proper function of good government, etc. The government left it up to the townships in the final analysis. But from 1907 on the argument continued, with a governmental commission stating flatly that "social security. . . . was an earned right." This led eventually to the adoption in 1913 (by a liberal government) of the old age Pension Law, the first real social reform act in Sweden. Up to then Sweden's record in social reform was sparse and entirely inadequate.[6]

Evaluating the direction and character of Swedish history in dealing with poverty is not easy. Poverty was indeed very present, but discussions of its extent, its cause, and its treatment by government are very ambiguous. In terms of our basic evaluative questions the answers seem fairly clear. First, the national government did not take an explicit role in caring for the poor until well into the 20th century. Second, the ideological debate over poverty was not apparent until the mid 19th century. And then it appeared very one-sidedly negative. Poverty was apparently dealt with in 90 percent rural Sweden, by the locals themselves. Third, the local townships were mentioned in the 19th century poor laws as the responsible units of government. Fourth, the role of the Lutheran Church is not clear, although the liberal opponents of governmental responsibility alluded to the care of the poor as more properly the role of religion and charity. Fifth, the role of elites, political and business, is by no means one in which they assumed responsibility for poor relief. Not until the 20th century as the parties debate the issue, and the labor unions press for effective social reforms, do we get some evidence of the conversion of elites to the cause of poor relief under governmental auspices. Hence, sixth, it is difficult to say reviewing Swedish history, as we have done briefly here, that there were clear lines of development or historical experiences, which would naturally lead to the strong system of poor relief adopted in Sweden after 1930.[7] The best we may be able to say is that there was an early equalitarian character to society, a nascent humanitarianism which later may have been relevant as Sweden moved towards social reform.

A Brief Summary of 19th Century German History on Poverty Relief

Germany is particularly important to our investigation because it was in a sense the pioneer in legislating social reforms. The German nation was established in 1871 composed of a variety of city-states and small kingdoms which had existed somewhat independently for some time. Otto Von Bismarck, the "Iron Chancellor" took over control with the Emperor William II. Less than fifteen years later he initiated his path breaking reforms.[8]

Before that in the earlier years of the Prussian system there had been rumblings of distress for the condition of the poor. Estimates suggested that up to 50% of the rural and urban underclass were living in the middle 19th century with no minimal protection from destitution and poverty.[9] Whatever relief there was available was provided by cities, towns, and rural groups. There were some institutions such as community dining halls, nurseries, hospitals, clinics, and house programs. There was some assistance for the poor but it was not well organized nor universal in availability. There was also some early Prussian state legislation, such as the limits on child labor (1839) and local insurance funds for the poor (1849 and 1854.) But the harsh panic of 1873 revealed the inadequacy of care.

Bismarck built on these efforts and was aware of their shortcomings. Historians report that he was fearful of the possibility of agitation and protest by those at the lower reaches of the society. And reputedly he also saw the early organizational institutions of the young socialists in the new Germany. In addition Bismarck felt that capitalism had left the state with the problem of poverty. Not all who wanted work could secure it under the new capitalism. Bismarck brought together the liberal economists and the conservatives in the enactment of his new legislation.

The basic point is that Bismarck decided that the central government should act to adopt and administer new programs. He began with the Health Insurance Law of 1884, and then followed with the Workmen's Compensation Act of 1885, and completed with his Old Age and Invalidity Pensions Act of 1889. These were all insurance programs, based on the principle of earnings related, compulsory contributions, on gross wages. Transfer payments were legislated for the latter two types of assistance (while health care costs were paid for as needed).

The Health Insurance Act covered from 5% at its inception to 25% of the population by World War I. So, many people were initially not covered. Similarly the Workmen's Compensation Act was revised so that employers had to carry most of the costs. As for old age pensions the coverage gradually increased to 15 million by 1908. Furthermore, the administration and operation of these reform plans was not really completely centralized. As for health insurance, for example, there were reported to be 20,000 insurance funds, occupationally specific, located in the municipalities.

Nevertheless, this pioneering attack on the welfare needs of their citizens in the 1880s must be considered very special. Certain key features stand out and must be remembered. The approach was the result of national government intervention. It was an attempt to set up a central state system, at least controlled by central state requirements. It was an obligatory system, applying to all who qualified. It was ideology-based, operating on the assumption that the state had to act to remedy the inadequacies and weaknesses of the capitalist system. Bismarck sought to forestall underclass agitation and protest. Scholars have referred to it also as a popular interventionist approach, appropriate to the German context in the latter part of the 19th century.[10]

As for poverty, Bismarck's reforms had an indirect effect. Assistance to the poor remained primarily the task of the local government officials. And leaders in politics, as well as businessmen and intellectuals, were divided as to how to alleviate poverty. They still argued the distinction between the "worthy" and "unworthy" poor. It would take a long time, until the years after World War II before a national reform action was taken to deal with this problem (of considerable magnitude in Germany after World War II). It was under Chancellor Adenauer and the Conservatives in 1961 that the first major action was taken to provide general assistance to the poor, called by some "the real German safety net" law![11]

The key questions which we use in evaluating these systems in their approach to poverty reform can also be applied to Germany. First, it is clear that at both the local and national levels there was concern about how to care for the poor, but Germany distinguished itself by developing reform programs nationally. However, this did not apply to poverty legislation, which had to wait until after World War II. Second, ideological discourse certainly occurred in the 19th century in several senses, particularly as a result of a concern over the rise of socialism. There were the beginnings of protests, partially attributed to the perceived consequences of capitalism. Bismarck, basically a conservative, was ironically the leader of the "progressive" social reform movement (later disillusioned because the socialists were not to be denied). Third, the role of the church in dealing with poverty is not adequately addressed by the historians reviewed by us for this analysis. Private charity groups did, however, do much to support a variety of institutions to help the poor locally. Fourth, local governments played a major role in what care the poor and destitute were provided, working with private groups, or administering national programs, or programs of their own. Fifth, one must remember that it was the conservative political

leaders (liber al-conservatives more properly) who underwrote the plans of
Bismarck, even while seeking to modify Bismarck's plans and to limit the
eligibility of those helped by these plans. And business leaders seemed also
to be mobilized in support. Finally, Germany in these early years is one case
where historical action in the 19th century set the stage for other national
programs (such as the 1927 Unemployment Insurance Act of the Weimar
period), eliminated in large part by the Nazis, but flourishing again in the
1950s and 1960s.

Notes

1. One good description of early history is found in Byron J. Nordstrom,
Scandinavia Since 1500 (Minneapolis, MN: University of Minnesota Press,
2000).

2. Nordstrom, *Scandinavia Since 1500*, 79.

3. Nordstrom, *Scandinavia Since 1500*, 113.

4. See Nordstrom, *Scandinavia Since 1500*, 231 for the emigration figures.
Between 1830 and 1930 three million Scandinavian left their homelands,
1.3 million of these were from Sweden.

5. Steven Koblik, *Sweden's Development From Poverty to Affluence, 1750–
1970*, (Minneapolis, Minn.: University of Minnesota Press, 1975), 10–11.

6. Koblik, *Sweden's Development*, 333.

7. It is important to remember that the Swedish party system developed
in early 20th century rather late. Universal suffrage was not adopted until
1921 (proportional representation in 1909). The early party opponents were
the Conservatives and Liberals with the Socialists emerging from the labor
movements in the Twenties.

8. See Peter J. Katzenstein, *Policy and Politics in West Germany: The
Growth of a Semisovereign State* (Philadelphia, Penn.: Temple University
Press, 1987) and Lewis J. Edinger, *Politics in Germany: Attitudes and
Processes*, (Boston, MA: Little Brown; 1968), for discussions about these
reforms. See also Allan Mitchell, *The Divided Path: The German Influence
on Social Reform in France After 1870*, (Chapel Hill, NC: North Carolina
Press, 1991).

9. Katzenstein, *Policy and Politics in West Germany*, 171.

10. See Mitchell, *The Divided Path*, 64–67.

11. Katzenstein, *Policy and Politics*, 178.

Part III

Final Observations: The 20th Century and Today

Chapter 12

The Finalization of Social Reform and Anti-Poverty Legislation in the United States and Western Europe In The 20th Century

Social reform legislation before World War I was just the prelude to a major expansion of such social policy in Western Europe after World War II. Soon after the war was over most of those countries adopted a "liberally" reconceptualized and very inclusive set of social reforms. By the late 1940s England, Sweden, and the Netherlands were well along in such discussion and legislative decisions, followed soon by the other three countries we discuss here (as well as Denmark, Norway, and Finland which we exclude here). All of these countries adopted detailed laws in the major areas of reform we referred to earlier: old age and disability pensions, health insurance, unemployment insurance, accident insurance, and anti-poverty social assistance (besides, of course, other types of special legislation). A brief review of this history in the post World War II period will clarify the context and action in each country.

In England the ground was laid by the appearance in 1942 of the Beveridge Report *Social Insurance and Allied Services*. This report was prepared for the English government during the war, laying out a set of principles which should guide such reform. The cooperation between the Labour and Conservative parties in Parliament at that time was significant. Among the principles of Beveridge which were accepted was that of "universality" (every family should be covered by such reform), the principle of "subsistence" (that "the amount of benefit adequate for physical subsistence"), and the principle of "national minimum" (that every person should receive assistance permitting him/her to have, through insurance, or despite the

lack of insurance, the means to meet minimal costs for living). [1] When
Labour came to power in 1945 (the Attlee Government), they adopted
by 1948 a series of social reform acts which incorporated these principles.
Among them were the provision of insurance benefits for sickness, disability, unemployment, old age, widowhood, maternity and the "death grant."
In 1948 this was accompanied by a law abolishing all aspects of the old
local government assistance system. Subsequent laws amended, improved,
and expanded the benefits provided in the legislation of 1948.

In the 50 years after World War II British party politics took several
turns. Perhaps the most major change was when Margaret Thatcher and
the Conservatives came to power in 1979, and for three consecutive periods
(after three conservative victories over the Labor party) remained in control
into the 1990s. While at first Prime Minister Thatcher initiated few changes
in social reforms, in latter periods her government did indeed seek to change
these policies. A "new right" political force had arrived in Britain and was
interested in returning to unalloyed capitalism. But it is interesting that in
the end the few changes adopted did not really alter the British reforms
drastically. Indeed, as Bochel concludes, after all these years "the central
role of the welfare state in Britain had not been seriously questioned." It
was supported strongly by MPs and the public, surveys revealed.

What is outstanding in the British case is that in the 20th century
Britain adopted and fairly well maintained a full-fledged social welfare system, with universal concern for all persons, including all of the poor. It is
an enlightened system, a humane system, and "one" with strong political
consensus at the mass level of the society and at the elite level. Especially
notable is the major role in, and strong support for, this system in a society
with a relatively low economic strength and development.

In Germany the context and sequence of events was quite different.
Germany had this great history of experimentation with social reforms
under Bismarck, in the 1880s. Then there was in a sense a major hiatus.
Under the Weimar Republic little happened, although an unemployment
insurance act was passed in 1927. Under the Nazis assistance programs
were left to localities and volunteer charity groups. After the war the new
Bonn Republic was faced with overwhelming problems, caring for refugees,
soldiers returning from action or from prisons, widows and orphans, etc. It
took some time to develop a coherent social reform program.[2]

Interestingly, it was under the chancellorship of Konrad Adenauer, leader
of the CDU (Christian Democratic Union) that social reforms were initiated. But, again, it was a consensus of parties' leaders which made these
reforms possible. In the elections from 1957 to 1972 the CDU had a larger
percentage of support than the SPD (46% to 42% on the average) but the
SPD was the larger party in 1972, and later also, in 1989. But it is inter-

esting that the parties did not fight intensely over reform policies, which Adenauer and the CDU initiated.

In 1957 the creation of a new old age pension system soon led to other acts. In 1961 they adopted a social security act and other laws, such as the new Labor Market Policy of 1969. A variety of other actions were taken, but only after considerable opposition not by the SPD but by the Bundesbank, the Finance Ministry, and some businessmen. But Adenauer prevailed, despite the business leaders, with the support of both parties. By 1979 14 million parents were getting child support payments, 12.9 million were getting social security payments, 6.1 million were receiving subsidized housing, 2.3 million were getting veterans benefits, 2.1 million were living on welfare, and 1.5 million received rent subsidies. This suggests the magnitude of the program of relief in West Germany.

There was considerable poverty in Germany for a long time after the war. The anti-poverty legislation of 1961 (amplified later, particularly in 1974,) helped provide relief. The German system was amazingly generous and responsive, in a bipartisan fashion, despite opposition. This helped to restore public confidence and to eventually contribute to Germany's post war resurrection.

In the Netherlands the process for the complete development of their social reform program was similar in some respects to that of the British. But there were also significant differences. The Dutch had adopted several reform laws before World War I as we indicated in our previous discussion. They had accident insurance (1901), aid for neglected children, a safe housing law, and an early Poor Law (1912). They had also in 1918 adopted major changes in their political system—extension of the right to vote, adoption of proportional representation, and a commitment of government support for all religious affiliated schools. In the interwar period the Dutch economy was doing very well until they finally felt the effects of the stock market collapse of 1929. By 1934 unemployment had declined and when the government decreased unemployment benefits, there was a series of protests. The government sought to deal with the problem by setting up a Labor Fund, to which they pledged 60 million guilders, but this did not in the end work out well. The rise of a Nazi party also exacerbated the situation. When World War II came to Holland, the society changed considerably under Nazi occupation, which gradually became less benign and more ugly in the last months before liberation.

Shortly after the war the country set to work on reconstruction. The election of 1946 was held which, as in the case of England, produced a government with a Labor party prime minister, the well-esteemed labor leader, Willem Drees. Drees Two major social reform laws were adopted under the four cabinets which Drees led as prime minister, 1948–1956: unemployment insurance and old age pensions (although an earlier act in 1947 had laid the ground work for the old age pension law). Some Dutch leaders attribute this early action, and also subsequent reform legislation, to the "understandings" which occurred in discussion groups at Nazi concentration "camps" in the Netherlands and in the Dutch resistance, over the type of society which should be created after the war. Whether true or not, considerable support across the party system was manifest for the successful reform program adopted.

A series of Dutch laws were enacted, aside from the two mentioned above: a widows and orphans act in 1959, child payments, 1962, major medical insurance in 1967, and special legislation for the handicapped in 1976. Other programs were added later.

Perhaps "the capstone" of the Dutch system was the anti-poverty law of 1965, called the General Assistance Act (*Algemene Bijstandswet*). This law, (actually adopted in 1963) required the national government to provide for every "subject" a "social minimum insurance" as a basic "right." Thus the government had the responsibility to see that every person had a decent standard of living. [3] This is one of the most direct statements ensuring that every individual and family shall have a safety net. One Dutch writer said after this law was passed, "finally with the adoption of the ABW the central government has accepted responsibility for the social welfare of all her subjects." Other laws were to be added later and new amendments to earlier social reform laws were also made, but the 1965 law made the commitment of governmental responsibility complete.

It is important to note that the passage of these laws from 1948 on occurred with the agreement and political support of most of the Dutch parties. In the 1948 Parliament, although Labour held the prime ministership, they shared control with a cabinet made up of representatives from three other parties: the Catholics (KVP), the Liberal Protestants (CHU) and the right of center Liberals (VVD). In the election to this Parliament Labor received 26% of the vote, the Catholics 31%, the CHU 9% and the VVD 8%. There obviously was a large consensus across party lines in support of the 1948 unemployment insurance bill.[4]

Similarly, in 1963, the non-labor political forces played a major role. The prime minister then was a Catholic, and the other parties in the cabinet were CHU, ARP (a conservative Protestant Reformed party), and VVD. Labor was not even in the cabinet at that time. In the election of 1963 preceding this Parliament 28% of the vote was for Labor, the Catholics had 32%, the ARP 9% and VVD 10%. It is true that although the Labour (PVDA) party played a major role in the post war period in pressing for social reform legislation, and Drees' role was particularly strong, Dutch elites in almost all the major parties believed in social reforms and revealed impressive consensus for implementing these reform objectives in Parliament.

Sweden's social welfare achievements in the 20th century are certainly a special case, a special story. It differed first in that it acted later than other countries—late because no action occurred before 1900. In the period before World War I its major laws were on factory safety (1912) and old age pensions (1913). When the Swedish government did act, after World War II, it adopted a most comprehensive, inclusive, and humanitarian social welfare system. What was unique was the dominance of the Social Democrats from 1932 to 1976, without a break in that control, which contributed to a philosophically coherent approach to social welfare. One must keep in mind, however, the size of the Social Democrats' vote during this period. This can be demonstrated in two ways:[5]

Table 12.1: Socialist Vote in Sweden 1932–1976

Party	Election Year Figures (Percentages)					
	1932	1936	1940	1956	1973	1976
Social Democrats	42	46	54	45	44	43
Socialist Bloc (left of center parties)	50	54	58	50	49	48

The consistency in the level of support for the "Left" and for the Social Democrats particularly, is indeed striking. However, if one is inclined to jump to the conclusion that it was only the Social Democrats who crafted and carried out the social reform program one would be somewhat wrong. The first reform, old age pensions, adopted in 1913 was pushed through by the Liberals, with the Social Democrats helping out. The consensual partisan character of Swedish politics is reflected also in the fact that when the Social Democrats lost the election in 1976 (and again in 1978) the conservatives continued to support these reforms.

Beginning in 1937, at least nine major social reform acts were passed in the period of "Left Bloc" control of the government. It began with maternity benefits (1937), and then was followed by children allowances (1948), health insurance (1955), the 45 hour work week (1960), new housing subsidies (1969), medical care compensation, simplified system (1970), dental care (1974), job safety requirements (1974), reduced pension age to 65 (1976). In addition, unemployment insurance begun in 1934 was extended in 1960. And finally a social assistance program which had been handled at the municipal level before the war, was taken over by national administrative agencies in the 50s and 60s. Thus, the Swedish anti-poverty program was completed. [6] "Social welfare commitments accumulated into an immense public sector in Sweden", according to Heclo and Madsen. Total public funding increased from 30% of GNP in 1960 to 66% by 1980.[7] The allocations alone for general public assistance (relief) increased from 17 million Kroner in 1956 to 161 million Kroner in 1962.[8]

The evaluations of the Swedish system have been very positive by most scholars. The politicians involved saw Sweden as a "people's home" which "touched a deep chord" among the Swedes early on. Social policy was seen "not just as a series of ad hoc reforms but as a way of re-creating a sharing, just community on a national basis." As the prime minister Tage Erlander said, Sweden was "a strong society" with its quality system of social services functioning "alongside a vigorously growing economy."[9] Sweden was more than "the middle way" as some had characterized it. Rather it was the strong, socially just society.

France's legislative history of social reform revealed a somewhat different pattern. As indicated earlier the ground work was laid before 1900 with an 1893 act providing medical aid to the poor and an 1898 act providing accident insurance. This was a partial response by France to Germany's actions under Bismarck.[10]

There was a long hiatus then until the 1930s depression came to France. Under a socialist prime minister in 1937 France responded to strong protests and demands from the growing labor unions by adopting a law providing for the 40 hour week, paid vacations, and public works employment.

France then entered the dark period of the war, the Nazi invasion of 1940, the creation of the collaborationist government of Pétain, and the eventual occupation of all of France after the allies won in North Africa. With the end of the war in 1945 France entered a new period. The third Republic was ended by a referendum in which over 90% of the public voted for a new system, which, after the adoption of a new constitution, was created in 1947. In between there was a provisional government under Charles de Gaulle. France went through a series of 20 or more cabinets in the ensuing decade, until in 1958 the 4th Republic was replaced by the 5th Republic with de Gaulle as President. As de Gaulle once said French politics was one of "perpetual political effervescence."[11] This was true particularly in the number and types of political parties which emerged and their rise and fall from one election to the next. At one time the Communists and Socialists ran the government, later excluded, only to return partially later under the 5th Republic. All cabinets were coalitions with many different parties.

Despite the great diversity, fluctuations, and "effervescence" of French politics, gradually progress was made on social reform. In 1945 a social security law was passed, in 1947 the first pension legislation. Later, when the Cold War set in, the Communists were split and other parties had difficulty pushing through social reforms. France was faced with the Catholic or "clerical question", the revolt in Algeria, difficulties with de Gaulle's dominance, and periodic economic declines—all factors which seemed to delay legislation. Eventually health insurance was adopted as well as unemployment insurance. And special legislation was passed to amend and expand earlier laws or replace them. In 1975 a law to take care of the handicapped was passed, in 1976 a law to help single parent families, in 1980 widow subsistence, and in 1984 improvements in unemployment insurance.

The capstone of the French social reform program, the anti-poverty law was passed in 1988. It was called the "RMI" law (*Revenu Minimum d'Insertion*), referring to the allocations of revenue to provide a "minimum" income to all persons, the aim being "insertion", or the integration of the poor into French society. There were requirements to be met—those eligible had to have residence in France for three years, exhaustion of their unemployment compensation after 60 months, and a commitment to look for work and willingness to work. They were to be provided medical insurance free, and grants for help with housing rents. A variety of administrators and social workers keep in touch with, and assist, these needy poor in every locality. Private charities and church welfare groups can, and do, participate in caring for these poor. But the key principle is that the government, the national government, accepts the basic responsibility for providing for the poor. Thus, in 1988, 23 years after the Dutch anti-poverty law was adopted, the French have committed themselves also to a basic obligation of the central government to provide poor relief.

In Belgium certain social reforms had been enacted before World War I as described earlier—laws concerning female and child labor (1889), accident insurance (1903), and early laws on sickness insurance and pensions (1911 and 1912). After World War I it was not until the thirties that further plans were discussed. A Plan for Labor was proposed and in 1936 after a conference of employees and employers legislation was passed providing for the 40 hour work week, paid vacations, and public subsidies for families for each child.[12]

In the meantime political organizations were developing and asserting themselves—several labor unions, a farmer's league, and several political parties. A new constitution in 1921 provided for proportional representation and expansion of the suffrage. The Belgium multi-party system characterized by significant ideological differences was functioning soon. The three main parties (Catholics, Socialists, and Liberals) competed closely. In fact, from 1918 to 1940 there were nine coalition cabinets including all three of these parties. Combined with conflict among interest groups, and the growing split in the country between the Walloon and the Flemish, plus a small German group—there was a multi-faceted context in which many bitter parliamentary battles occurred from the 1920s on. Yet some reforms were passed even before World War II. But from the period in May, 1940 when the Nazis took over Belgium until the late forties and fifties, very limited reforms were possible.

The parties changed their names after the war, to the Catholic Peoples Party (CVP), the Belgium Socialist Party (BSP), and the smaller Liberal Party. Long discussions and many arguments over reforms took place. The CVP and the BSP displaced each other several times in power in the government during this period. The legislation which was adopted represented compromises, particularly in the administration of the social reform laws adopted. In 1944, after the Nazis left, a new wage earners employment insurance act was passed. Very soon thereafter, in 1954 and in succeeding years a series of reforms were adopted including health insurance, disability insurance, and refinements of the social security and unemployment insurance legislation. It was then that the responsibility for the operation of these laws was assumed by the national government (formerly they were in the hands of local authorities). The social organizations who had created special insurance programs (by unions, charitable societies, etc.), were permitted to continue these insurance programs but under governmental supervision. Finally, in 1974 the Belgians also adopted a basic anti-poverty

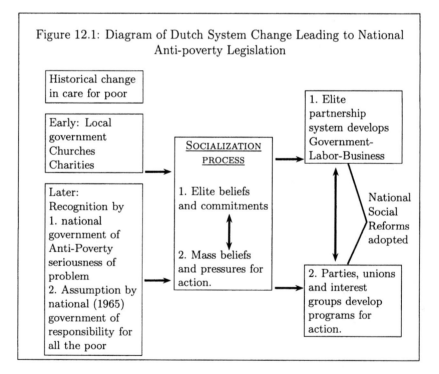

Figure 12.1: Diagram of Dutch System Change Leading to National Anti-poverty Legislation

law, following the previous law of the Dutch in 1965, stipulating that every Belgian citizen had a right to a guaranteed, minimum income or "safety net." This in a sense declared and certified what had already existed in some form for some time. And this "General Assistance" ("Algemene Bijstand") became a special provision. In 1998 the government reported having spent over 55 million Belgian francs on this type of poor relief.[13]

This completes our historical updating of the welfare reform history of the six West European countries (including Britain) in our study. In all six we find very similar types of legislation. Above all, for our purposes it is important to note that all of them adopted legislation providing for poor relief in legislation which specified that the national government assumed responsibility for taking care of the poor, assuring each individual and family a minimally decent standard of living.

The historical paths and processes which brought these countries to a national commitment to poor relief were varied. But it seems clear that history was relevant, that socialization of elites and masses was critical, and that parties and other institutions played major roles. The accompanying diagram (see Figure 12.1) of one way to look at what was happening in Western Europe, using the Netherlands as a prime example, attempts to summarize the way in which these factors worked together to lead to national comprehensive anti-poverty legislation. Unfortunately, this historical process was never fulfilled in the United States.

United States Social Reform in the Twentieth Century

The United States pattern of governmental care for the underclass and the social reforms related to that was quite different than in Western Europe. First, of course, our legislation at the national level came late. Although some American states began in the 1900s to pass laws regarding working conditions for women and children, and workmen's compensation laws were introduced before World War I, no national laws were enacted early. The United States national government assumed no responsibility for social reform. It took the Depression in the thirties to force action by the President and Congress. After Franklin Roosevelt's election in 1932, it became quite clear that the millions of unemployed had to be helped. At first the "dole" was used and then Roosevelt realized this was both inadequate and degrading as assistance to the poor. Congress then created the National Youth Act (NYA), the Civil Works Adminstration (CWA)—later called the Public Works Administration (PWA), the Civilian Conservation Corps (CCC), and the Works Progress Administration (WPA) as a public works approach for the immediate relief of the unemployed poor. In addition Congress passed the Housing Act of 1934 and also provided funds for the states to set up employment offices. The Civil Works Administration provided jobs to 4.2 million in 1934, and the Public Works Administration three million by 1936. The Federal Emergency Relief Administration (FERA) in a two year period provided over 3 billion dollars in direct relief. Not all of the 10 million unemployed were taken care of but the majority were helped by these public sector jobs. These agencies were continued into the Forties, but when World War II began for the United States they were really no longer needed, and by 1942 were in process of being eliminated. The demands of the war provided adequate jobs for most people who wanted them.[14]

At the same time as we were providing employment relief to the poor, we also adopted one of the most significant social reform acts of the century–the Social Security Act of 1935. This was passed in August, 1935 by overwhelming majorities of both Democrats and Republicans in Congress. This law is the foundation for the United States old age pension legislation, as well as providing for unemployment insurance, and, thirdly, including provisions for assistance to dependent children and the disabled. It was decided that the old age pension system would be administered by the national government, while the unemployment insurance program would be administered by the states. It initially applied to only a small percent of the elderly but was expanded to all eventually. As Skocpol put it, this 1935 Act has turned out to be "the closest approximation the United States would achieve to a modern welfare state."[15] The program for the elderly poor was to be financed by worker and employer contributions. Amendments were made to the law subsequently, to include "survivors", disabled workers, and for those retired persons needing medical care. And the inclusion of people over the years, as well as the increase in benefits, have made the system a center piece of our social reform system.

Unfortunately the United States made no effort to enact two other types of social reforms at this time, health insurance for everyone and an anti-poverty commitment. West European nations, as we saw, did eventually enact both of those. We made more progress after World War II during Johnson's administration in the Sixties providing medical aid to the elderly and the poor, as well as the food stamp program. But this medical aid was not comprehensive. So today we still suffer from major gaps in our social welfare program.

During World War II poor relief lapsed, and the only piece of legislation which was adopted was the "GI Bill" in 1944, to provide extensive employment, housing, business, health, and educational assistance to the millions of veterans. This law was administered by the Veteran's Affairs administration. Also, a special agency was created in Washington to study what our post war social provision needs would be. This was the National Resources Planning Board (1943). Roosevelt hoped that with the Democrats in control of Congress other legislation advocated under the New Deal would be possible. But the support for these ideas did not materialize, due to the opposition of business many Republicans and southern Democrats to such legislation. In the late Forties and in the Fifties there were many proposals for new reforms, but little was adopted. President Truman worked very hard to get Congress to act on more than one proposal. Under Kennedy and Johnson's "War on Poverty" in the Sixties, there were new efforts. President Harry Truman fought hard for social reform legislation both before and after his 1948 election. His full employment bill, committing the government to provide a job for everyone who could, and would work, was defeated first. And then his national health insurance proposal met with strong opposition by the American Medical Association and conservatives in Congress. These were major blows to Truman's proposals. The conservative coalition was strengthened after the 1950 elections and health insurance had no chance of survival.[16]

Under Presidents Kennedy and Johnson there were new efforts. The following actions by Congress are perhaps the most notable.

1961 –(AFDC)–Aid to Families with Dependent Children, an extension of the 1935 Aid to Dependent Children (ADC): administered by the states.

1964 –Food Stamps adopted early but expanded in 1974–For help to low income families.

1965 –Medicaid–to provide medical assistance to low income people who are aged, blind, or disabled, administered by states under federal guidelines. Adopted along with Medicare despite strong Republican opposition.

1965 –Medicare–originally aid for the elderly poor. Adopted despite considerable lobbying efforts against it by insurance companies and the American Medical Association.

1972 –Supplemental Security Income (SSI)–effective in 1974. A guaranteed income for the aged, disabled and blind. This act came closest, for these special groups, to the guaranteed minimum standard of living laws adopted for all citizens in Europe. Adopted under the Nixon Administration.

1975 –Earned income Tax Credit (EITC)–a program for low income wage-earners, it subsidized families who work but at low wage levels. Adopted under the Ford Administration.

1988 –Family Support Act–A modestly funded act that was aimed at getting people off welfare, provide "job" training, etc. Limited applicability and use. It led to the 1996 Act under Clinton.

1996 –Personal Responsibility Work Opportunity Reconciliation Act (PRWORA)–The so called "welfare to work" law which allocates funds to the states to administer rules by which those on welfare are required to work and thus leave welfare. Passed under Clinton Administration with Republican control of Congress. Expired after five years and renewed by Congress each year.

Thus, we can see that several major and varied social reform measures have been passed since the 1935 Social Security Act. These deal with, and provide, assistance for people at considerable cost to the government, even though some are insurance programs. A recent study collected data on the spending for these welfare programs over the years. Here is a brief summary of these expenditures (in billions of 1990 dollars).[17]

Social reform program expenditures (billions of dollars)

	Year	1960	1970	1980	1992
A	Cash assistance: (AFDC, EITC, etc.)	22.3	36.5	47.9	63.6
B	In-kind assistance: food stamps, housing, energy, Medicaid, etc	4.8	25.6	84.3	154.9
C	Social Insurance: old age, disability, unemployment, workers compensation, Medicare	65.2	141.8	301.0	461.1
D	Educational and Training: head start, higher education, student loans	0.5	13.0	33.1	23.8
	Total spending as a % of GNP	4.4	6.7	10.8	12.9

The United States has obviously in the last 70 years sought to deal with selected problems with its social welfare legislation. It has spent a great deal. Yet, comparatively one study showed we are not doing as well as we should. Using GDP, this study finds that in 1990 the United States spent 11.5% compared to 23.5% for France, 21.2% for Sweden, 19.3% for West Germany, 13.7% in the United Kingdom. Only Japan among modern democracies spends less than we do![18] Despite all this expenditure, however, we still have 37 million Americans living below the poverty level and 46 million with no health insurance.

It is important to remember in this comparative look at social welfare and anti-poverty relevant legislation in the twentieth century, how the United States differs. Our legislative record has been episodic, even sporadic, after a very late start. After 1935 nothing happened until 1961, 1964, 1965. After Johnson's presidency, no major pieces of legislation (except perhaps for SSI and EITC) were even presented to Congress until the Clinton presidency. And then, after threatening to veto it, he reluctantly did sign the 1996 Act which was not an enlightened piece of legislation. In all this we kept avoiding comprehensive help for the poor, while in Europe much legislation was adopted from the 1940s–1960s on, including (or leading up to) a comprehensive commitment to help all the poor. But not in the United States.

Notes

1. In this report we have used among others, Victor George's, *Social Security and Society* (London: Routledge and Kegan Paul, 1973) and Hugh Bochel, *Parliament and Welfare Policy* (Aldershot, England:Dartmouth Publishing Company, 1992).

2. Among the German studies, we have used particularly Peter J. Katzenstein, *Policy and Politics in West Germany: The Growth of a Semisovereign State* (Philadelphia, PA: Temple University Press, 1987) and Lewis J. Edinger, *Politics in Germany: Attitudes and Processes* (Boston, MA: Little Brown; 1968)

3. L. Frank Van Loo, *Arm in Nederland 1850–1990* (Meppel, the Netherlands: Boom, 1992), 16.

4. For these election and cabinet data, see Rudy B. Andeweg and Galen A. Irwin, *Dutch Government and Politics* (London: the Macmillen Press, 1993), 105 and 119.

5. Sten Berglund and Ulf Lindstrom, *The Scandinavian Party System(s)* (5), (Lund, Sweden: Studentlitt, 1978), 85–86.

6. See Hugh Heclo and Henrik Madsen, *Policy and Politics in Sweden: Principled Pragnatism* (Philadelphia: Temple University Press, 1987), 7–8, 154–173.

7. Heclo and Madsen, *Policy and Politics*, 165.

8. Carl G. Uhr, *Sweden's Social Security: an Appraisal of its Economic Impact in the Postwar Period*, (Washington, DC: U.S. Department of Health, Education, and Welfare, Social Security Administration, Office of Research and Statistics; U.S. Government. Printing Office", 1966), 121.

9. Heclo and Madsen, *Policy and Politics*, 158

10. References used here for France include Eric Tournier, *Économie et Société Françaises Depuis 1973* (Paris: Nathan, 1999); John D. Stephens, *Transition From Capitalism to Socialism* (Urbana, IL: University of Illinois Press, 1986).

11. Quoted in Roy Pierce, *French Politics and Political Institutions* (New York: Harper & Row, 1968), 1.

12. Among the many books on Belgium, we found useful I.C.H. Blom and Emiel Lamberts, *History of the Low Countries* (New York: Berghahn Books, 1999; and Herman Deleeck, *De Architectuur Van De Welvaartsstaat Opnieuw Bekeken* (Leuven, Belgium, ACCO 2001).

13. Deleeck, *De Architectuur Van De Welvaartsstaat*, 449–450.

14. Useful studies of the United States are many. References used here were Sheldon H. Danziger, Gary D. Sandefur and Daniel H. Weinberg eds.*Confronting Poverty: Prescriptions for Change* (Cambridge, MA: Harvard University Press, 1994). Theda Skocpol, *Social Policy in the United States: Future Possibilities in Historical Perspective* (Princeton, NJ: Princeton University Press, 1995), Harrell Rodgers, *American Poverty in a New Era of Reform* (Armonk, NY: E. Sharpe, 2000), Charles Noble, *Welfare As We Knew It* (New York: Oxford University Press, 1997).

15. Skocpol, *Social Policy in the United States*, 136.

16. Monte M. Poen, *Harry S. Truman Versus the Medical Lobby* (Columbia, MO: University of Missouri Press, 1979).

17. Danziger, *Confronting Poverty*, 57.

18. Danziger, *Confronting Poverty*, 81.

Chapter 13

Conclusion: What Are The Prospects?

It is time now, in the 21st century, for the United States to finally resolve this national poverty problem. We have sought a solution to this crisis by adopting several different legislative efforts over time. But the problem is as great today as 50 years ago 12.7% of our population (17% of our children) are living in poverty. This was also the same percentage as in the early 1960s. This is unacceptable and shameful. We need to observe and follow the example of our West European colleagues who developed successful programs for dealing with poverty. Today they continue their struggle to support the poor despite economic decline. One may well argue that ours is a democracy emphasizing individualism, that each person is responsible for himself or herself. But we also like to think about ourselves as a humanitarian democracy. Independence under American capitalism has lead to great wealth for a few and less for the many underprivileged. As Franklin D. Roosevelt said in his 1937 inaugural address to Congress, "The test of our progress is not whether we add more to the abundance of those who have much; it is whether we provide enough for those who have too little."

It is necessary to keep in mind the causes of poverty and the reasons for our failures to deal with it effectively. And then we need to search for our ways to eliminate poverty.

In the evaluation of the prospects for a more comprehensive poverty program, we can pose a series of questions, and try to answer them. The first question is to what extent has the inadequacy of state aids been responsible for our failure? As we stated in Chapter One comparative data reveal that in West Europe countries state aid has played a major role in reducing poverty while this is much less true in the United States. The gap in state aid is considerable, up to 60% in West Europe and 27% in the United States. The recent economic decline in Europe and the United States has been met in Europe by some reduction in benefits but with the maintenance of a "safety net" for most of the poor. In the United States, we are still arguing in Congress how to change our 1996 law to improve our relief for our poor who have no real "safety net." Thus the large variance in assistance to the poor, between the United States and Western Europe continues.

What have we learned from our study of the history of these seven countries, and the functioning of their contemporary systems which help us understand the probable causes for this variance? That is our second, key, question. It is clear that the American experience with poverty was comparable up to the late 19th century, when it diverged in major respects: (1) the distinction between "worthy" and "unworthy" poor persisted far into the 20th century in the United States, while Europeans abandoned this dichotomy, and viewed the poor despite their incapacities as fellow citizens, probable victims of the system, and worthy of assistance; (2) Europeans considered poor relief a public function (although often supported partly by private charities, but under governmental supervision), while in the United States this was never completely accepted. While in the colonial period city governments assumed control, in the later period this was not strictly adhered to; (3) the Western European systems eventually accepted the concept and ideology of national governmental commitment to a responsibility to care for all the poor, while the United States obviously never has accepted that approach to poor relief.

Further, our analysis of the national political elite systems of these countries, particularly the character of the legislative elites, reveals major differences in orientations, backgrounds, recruitment, and beliefs between the American and West European systems. In addition the role of business establishments and leaders is strikingly different in these European countries than in the United States. This has led to a great disparity in the beliefs of political leaders in their capacity and willingness to deal with, and provide for, the alleviation of poverty. These differences looked at in conjunction with the different historical path which the United States took, may provide us with some enlightenment as to why we have been so slow to address the poverty problem as frontally as the Europeans have.

We learned also, or were reminded, by our analysis that we have on occasion mobilized a majority vote to pass social reform legislation linked to helping the poor. In the 1930s (particularly with the passage of the Social Security Act of 1935), and in the 1960s with the three major pieces of social reform legislation, we were successful. But over the years we have also learned how difficult it is to mobilize a national (Congressional) majority for such legislation. The failures under Presidents Truman and

Kennedy are most notable. We noted also how, since Lyndon Johnson's presidency, little has been done by Democrats or Republicans in Congress to reduce poverty. It reduced poverty in the short run by 2000 but since then poverty has reached again a high. One may argue that the 1996 Act represents progress, but it certainly has not reduced poverty in the long run.

Actually if we review the list of legislative decisions on social reform which were made, it is clear that despite the institutional and political obstacles, much was achieved. For some idea of the magnitude of our support for the poor, note the data in Table 13.1

Table 13.1: Samples of Financial Support for the Poor

1. Food Stamps:	1972	1996
Expenditures ($ millions)	1,871	25,494
Persons participating (millions)	11.1	26.9
2. Medicaid:		
Expenditures ($ millions–federal and state)	8,434	16,963
3. SSI–Supplementary Security Income:	1974	1996
Annual payments ($ millions–1996 dollars)	16,696	28,252
Number of beneficiaries (millions)	3.996	6.614
4. Earned Income Tax Credit	1975	1996
Number of families receiving credit (millions)	6.215	18.692
Total amount of credit ($ millions)	$1,250	$25,058

It is clear that the United States government in recent years has at least doubled the funds spent, and for certain types of assistance have tripled. In a variety of ways we have made attempts at providing some poor relief. One may well ask then, "Why isn't poverty decreasing?" A close analysis of who is helped (and through what programs) reveals that fewer people are removed from poverty than one would have expected. Rodgers[1] reports the results of such an analysis from 1979 to 1996 (asking how many persons were removed from poverty as a result of social assistance, means—tested cash assistance, food and housing benefits, and earned income tax credits) and concludes that in 1996 only 26,690 persons went off poverty in that year as a result of these programs.[2] Clearly a result like that in a society with 37 million living in poverty is not impressive. It is illusory.

This leads to our third question—in what specific way have we failed in our anti-poverty efforts, compared to Western Europe? The answers are both simple (and immediate) and profound (long term and historic). One reason is, of course that we do not spend as much of our great wealth to help

the poor as we should, and as other countries do. A recent analysis found
in Danziger and Haveman's book *Understanding Poverty* documents the
comparative difference. If one calculates the % of GDP spent for welfare
benefits (for other than the elderly) for the poor we find the following
percentages by country:[3]

Netherlands	14.1	United Kingdom	9.4
Sweden	13.8	Germany	8.4
Belgium	12.1	France	10.7
		United States	3.7

These are data for the late Nineties. And they tell the story clearly—we
don't spend proportionately what we should on the care for our poor, not
as much as we can (remember, we are a great economic power) and should.

A second obvious reason for our failure to decrease poverty is that we
think that if we get people off "welfare" (the bad word in America) we will
get them off the poverty list. It isn't so. In 1996 we passed our most recent
Act, giving money to the states, to deal with poverty, and requiring them
to get people off welfare. The states now boast that they did that—a 50%
decline in the number of people on welfare. But that didn't mean they were
not living in poverty! What a delusion for us! Getting off welfare and then
getting some kind of job doesn't mean getting over the poverty line. What
we have now as a result is many more "working poor" or jobless. Again,
what an illusory approach to dealing with poverty.[4]

A third reason for increased poverty is that we refuse to deal with job
training and more education for the poor. We have known for a long time
that this is a big part of the problem and we don't do enough. We tried to
do more of this under the 1996 Act but it is minimal, varies greatly by state,
and obviously not enough. One scholar argues that "the basic answer" to
poverty "is education", those with more education make the real income
gains. Of course we know this, but how well have we applied the knowledge
to the poverty problem? We also know that a major difficulty exists for
the single parent family when there is no financial provision for child day
care. Even now there are proponents in Congress (Democrats) pressing for
a revision of the 1996 law by adding financial support for child care, as
well as job training. That we are still arguing this point at the beginning
of the 21st century is indeed amazing. Recognizing that American family
structure has changed radically in the United States in recent years (from
1961 to 1992 the % of single-parent families with children increased from
10% to almost 25%).[5] We need to adjust to this reality and adapt our
legislation to it.[6]

These are simple reasons why we have failed to deal well with poverty.
Every intelligent observer of American society knows this; every member
of Congress must know that these are the immediate reasons. (It's not

because poor people are lazy, on drugs, cheaters, unworthy, and hopeless). Other societies (such as we have studied) have all realized that the poor are worthy of help, that many of them are victims of the system (the capitalist system mainly), and that these poor citizens deserve relief and assistance. In England, Belgium, Sweden, Holland, France and Germany their governments have all accepted the challenge and developed legislation based on a keen awareness of the difficulties the poor face in modern societies. They continue to struggle to save all of them if possible.

Our Fourth Question: What Does It Take To Get Comprehensive Poverty Reform?

If we are to get reform in the United States we need major comprehensive legislation, not just partial, sporadic, weak efforts. To get this we need representatives in Washington, presidential and congressional with more humane perspectives on the problem of poverty! We need the United States Congress to declare that they accept full responsibility for providing a decent standard of living for all the poor. How do we get this? It is obviously a long process requiring much intellect and courage. Let us look at how West European governments got this. What seem to be the key elements in their success?

1. First we need a high level discourse by intellectuals, legislators, business leaders, labor leaders, religious leaders, media leaders, social workers, etc. to engage in what I would call "outrage discourse" about the degrading state of the poor in the United States. That's what happened in Europe. Take England, for example. Throughout the 19th century, there was a continual public debate on the 1834 Poor Law and its degradations. Conservative politicians like Disraeli denounced it. A prominent business leader, Booth , did his own study of poverty in London and published 17 volumes in his report. Social workers like Sidney and Beatrice Webb debated the issue constantly. And finally the government woke up and appointed a Royal Commission in 1903 to investigate. That produced results! Similarly the Dutch leaders who had been put in special "concentration" camps by the Nazis during the war, and those in the Resistance, reportedly debated at length the type of society they wanted after the war. These were a wide variety of leaders—and they began to agree, despite their different political affiliations, on the social reforms they wanted. After the war they pressed for action. Outrage discourse can help develop an agenda, and then press for action.

2. A comprehensive plan to meet the remaining social reform needs of our society and the different types of legislation needed to do the job.

We have in the past years only partially acted if at all. We need an overall blueprint for legislative action. The English Beveridge Plan developed during World War II by representatives of the main parties is an example. The Swedish Social Plan is another excellent example, as is also the Dutch Plan. A comprehensive set of principles and objectives needs to be discussed and adopted.

3. Congress should adopt a resolution accepting responsibility for providing a decent standard of living for the poor, just as six West European nations have done. We can call this the "safety net" resolution. The requirements for receiving such help should be specified, including a means-test.

4. In the follow-up financial provision we should keep in mind that we already allocate 16.9 billion dollars each year to the states, plus allocating for food stamps, Social Security, EITC, etc. Since this legislation will no doubt be administered by the states, we should set federal standards for providing assistance, so that the wide range of financial support by states would no longer be allowed. The gap between low income and the poverty threshold should be closed so far as possible. No poor person or household should be deprived. Above all, there should be no time limits on welfare.

5. Three obvious difficulties today are lack of jobs, lack of education, and lack of child support. The government needs to do much more to provide jobs, public jobs, to those who can work. Job training should be provided, particularly in the large cities, and child care for working single family mothers.

6. Finally, as has been advocated in Sweden, we should consider setting up a Community Poor Relief and Service program, by act of Congress. The aim would be to organize and centralize in each community the poor relief system. It would work with the local city council to pool the voluntary services of interested and caring people, with the efforts of churches, charities, and social welfare workers, so that no poor person would suffer from lack of advice and necessary help. As in colonial days, the city would be the focus for the local administration of the national poverty program.

If we are to match the West European systems we need to adopt a basic Poor Law which includes the above elements. It has to be done by the President and Congress working closely with business leaders and labor leaders, similar to the "partnership plan" in Europe.

An Evaluation of our Capacities for Such Action—Our Fifth Question

What is the potential for such action by our American political leaders? Are they ignorant of the state of the poor, of the failure of our policies? Are they perhaps knowledgeable, but not concerned? Have they no desire as representatives of the people to deal with this social problem? Or are they just not compassionate, generous, or humane when it comes to spending for the American "underclass"?

One hears very little these days from the chambers of the elites in Congress or from the President about the needs of the poor. We spend $350 billion on tax cuts, probably $300 billion or more on the war, $15 billion on the problem of AIDS in Africa, but we just cut out funds for poor children in the tax cut bill, and have left the revision of the 1996 "Welfare Law" on the shelf. Under five presidents—Carter, Reagan, Bush I, Clinton, Bush II, covering almost 30 years, we have not had one new (and successful) decent, piece of anti-poverty legislation adopted. What kind of elites do we have in this system of ours, in either party, Democratic or Republican? Where is the intelligence, the moral outrage, the integrity, the vision? Do we have a crisis of representation, a failure in elite responsiveness to public problems?

There are, one may argue, profound reasons for the failure of American leaders to act. Lack of basic belief, or absence of basic values, which would naturally motivate a leader to be humanely involved in dealing with the miseries of the poor. Our colonial history did not manifest this lack of humane values. In our review of this early American history we discovered that in the pre-Revolutionary period from 1700 on, in cities like Boston, New York, and Philadelphia there was a considerable concern for the poor, and much effort by the church and by local city governments to take care of the poor, in a variety of ways. Long ago in the country there was an active conscience by leaders, rich and middle class, to be aware of poverty and to work hard to reduce it. They may have been very "individualistic" in their value orientations in some respects, but so far as poverty was concerned they worked collectively to help the poor. There seems to be a great "historic gap" between the 18th century's community concern and action dealing with poverty, and the 20th century in this regard, at least until the Depression forced governmental action.

It is interesting to reflect on what it would take to revive a sense of humaneness in our national leaders—in Presidents and members of Congress. From our review of the actions of these leaders in the 20th century and recently (after 2000), what conclusions would one arrive at? Let us look at a few case studies. It is interesting that the biography of President Theodore Roosevelt suggests that when about 1905 he visited the slums of New York he was so shocked that he returned to Washington vowing that he would do something to improve the working and living conditions of those in such abject poverty. And he did propose something to Congress, but no action emerged and after he lost the 1912 election with his Bull Moose Party he observed that he was sorry he would not have the opportunity to do more—to implement the liberal social reform platform of his new party, which had been defeated.

President Franklin D. Roosevelt, though an aristocrat, seems to have been innately more sensitive to the problems of the poor, reinforced no doubt by the long lines of the unemployed, hungry people waiting for food at the "soup kitchens." He provided not only food, but millions of jobs for many of the unemployed through agencies like the WPA. He then engineered his Social Security Act through Congress in 1935. The advisors around FDR, including his wife Eleanor, no doubt had a strong supporting influence on him. But it was FDR who had the humane values and motivations to press for action necessary to deal with poverty. Thus, the pressure of the economic crisis, the plight of the poor masses, personal experiences, family upbringing, and ideological commitment—all could drive a president to act. Plus, of course, a keen awareness of the problems of society and a strong sense of duty to do something about them were necessary if effective action was to occur. And, in FDR's case, he persuaded over 80% of Republicans in Congress and over 90% of Democrats to support his 1935 Social Security Act.

President John Kennedy is an interesting study in this light. Also from an aristocratic and well-to-do family, he was at first very uneasy in developing his program, primarily because he was elected with such a miniscule majority in 1960. His early actions were very favorable to business, including large corporation tax cuts and his early decision not to increase spending for social reform purposes. His liberal instincts were subdued—no civil rights actions until 1963. But Kennedy's concern for the poor was finally also revived in that year. He asked his Council of Economic Advisors (CEA) what it would cost to fund an anti-poverty program to eliminate poverty. The CEA told him that "direct transfers could remove all the poor from poverty for $11 billion a year."[7] This led to Kennedy's commitment shortly before his assassination to act on this recommendation. Thus, Kennedy, the reluctant politician slow to act, eventually became a president who advocated the elimination of poverty. His humane conscience prevailed. Lyndon Johnson, Kennedy's successor, went forward with Kennedy's plan, and his own, legislative "War on Poverty." He fought hard in the Congress to get his Medicare and Medicaid bills adopted, major initiatives to care for the elderly and non-elderly poor. Johnson was the great politician who put his skills in dealing with Congress to work to achieve great victories in a variety of policy areas, pursuing doggedly his strong commitment to solving America's social problems.

These "case studies" of FDR, Kennedy, Johnson and others are very suggestive, and lead us back to the main question—what conditions, forces, or influences produce a humane president or legislator? We are left with a variety of answers. "Context" is obviously relevant, but not necessarily determinative. Values, beliefs, and a proper sense of priority are also critical conditions. The conditions that prevail in Washington at a particular time may be critical, contributing to probable political defeat or probable victory depending on the party strength and alignments (Southern Democrats who were conservative were often a thorn in the side of a Democratic president who wanted to act). The strength of business and corporations in Washington could constrain liberal presidents, as it did eventually (from 1937 on) for FDR, for Kennedy in the early years, and for Johnson also in the early years. But it could not absolutely and finally defeat all social reform legislation. In the final analysis superior to all such contextual considerations are the ideological mind-sets of the leaders. If they were "believers" and believers with a will, and a set of humane perceptions on society, they would dare to act, and they would often be successful. That is how we got those few social reform pieces of legislation on poverty, spread out over many years. Unfortunately the American political recruitment process for president and Congress does not often provide a set of elites in Washington with a sense of moral and social responsibility strong enough to influence the behavior of such elites in power.

What produces a humane president or humane member of Congress? Look at the list of poverty relevant actions adopted—from 1935 to 1996. Depending on what one would call a "major" social reform action, one could arrive at possibly eight (excluding extensions and expansions of acts already in existence). These are listed in Table 13.2.

In the long list of presidents in the 20th century and into the 21st century, most of them had no interest at all. Some did try to adopt more legislation. Harry Truman introduced a health insurance bill but it never got past the Ways and Means Committee. As we noted John Kennedy died before his anti-poverty proposal was acted on. Interestingly, Richard Nixon supported a variety of extensions of welfare aid initiated in earlier presidencies. And he was only one of two Republican presidents to get action on a new piece of anti-poverty legislation. Some presidents (as Reagan) worked actively against such legislation—poverty actually increasing during the early years of his administration. And our current Republican president has sought to revise the 1996 Act with new strict requisites for state aid to the poor, while signing a tax cut bill in 2003 which actually fails to help 6.5 million low income families with children in poverty, while

Table 13.2: Successful Anti-Poverty Laws in the United States

Legislation	Year	President
Social Security Act	1935	F.D. Roosevelt
AFDC*	1950	H. Truman
Food Stamp Program	1964	L. Johnson
Medicaid	1965	L. Johnson
Medicare	1965	L. Johnson
Supplemental Security Income	1972	R. Nixon
Earned Income Credit	1975	G. Ford
PRAWOR** Act	1996	W. Clinton

*Aid to Families with Dependent Children
**Personal Responsibility and Work Opportunity Reconciliation

giving over 60% of tax cut gains to the top wealthy families.

Thus, one may conclude in answering the same basic question—how can we produce more humane (and effective) anti-poverty legislators in Washington? Do not rely on a Republican president to initiate such major, new legislation; since 1900 only three of eleven have shown any interest (T. Roosevelt–Ford–Nixon). One exception to the negativism of the Republican party is the case of the Americans with Disabilities Act (ADA) which was passed in 1990 during the term of the first President Bush. This Act was a major landmark in enhancing equal opportunities for people with disabilities. The chances are better with a Democrat as President–five of seven since 1900 have at least initiated anti-poverty relevant legislation. And we cannot count on Republican majority in support of such legislation to assist the poor. Only in 1935 when the poor were in the streets–only then under the pressure of a Democratic president did a majority of both parties support the Social Security Act. The Republicans rejected Truman's efforts and opposed Kennedy and Johnson in his "war on poverty." The Republicans don't like to vote in favor of poor relief.

There can be no doubt that our elites have failed to deal adequately with one of the most basic problems at the mass level of society–poverty. We did pass several important laws relevant to that problem, but we never have really finished the job. And that is particularly unfortunate because study after study reveals that the public supports anti-poverty legislations. In one of Gallup's surveys almost 70% of American adults agreed with the statement: "the federal government has a deep responsibility for seeing that the poor are taken care of, that no one goes hungry, and that every person achieves a minimum standard of living."[8]

We have had for a long time a critical under-representation or misrepresentation of the American public's attitude and belief on the poverty question. We may well ask how representative are the elites in our democracy? Our leaders in Washington are supposed to be aware of key issues (such as poverty), concerned about the issue, and responsive to it. Since 1935, on the poverty question we have not seen much of that responsiveness by the leaders of both parties. In 1935 when the Social Security Act was adopted, Gallup reported 89% of the public was in favor of such action. Congressmen supported the adoption of that Act. Since then the public continues to favor federal government assumption of responsibility for caring for all the poor, but only occasionally has a majority of Congress approved, and then when Democrats are in charge. Studies of political representation produced mixed results when they analyze Western democracies.[9] But on the poverty issue (as on social reform policies) in Britain and Western Europe, parliamentary leaders early reflected the desire of their constituents by adopting the necessary legislation with strong majorities. Is it probable that American elites are more responsive to the more affluent sector of the electorate than to "the underclass"?

The American system is often judged as a representative democracy whose political leadership kept in touch with public opinion through frequent elections. For a variety of reasons that is not always so. Research shows that for possibly 60% of major policies adopted in Washington, leaders' decisions "follow" public opinion.[10] That is a fairly high percentage, but much of the legislation can not be characterized as "following" public opinion. Certainly our anti-poverty legislation has not "followed" public opinion. Western European elites seem much more in tune with their public on social welfare questions.[11]

What then is to be done? As soon as we have a large enough number of humane politicians in Washington, Congress and the President should adopt a "responsibility resolution", similar to the type of resolution adopted in the Parliaments of our Western European friends. This resolution should state "the government accepts the responsibility for seeing that every citizen (and permanent resident) of the United States lives at or above the poverty line and has at least a decent standard of living." This is what the Dutch government committed to in 1965, preceded by the British in the 1940s, Sweden in the 1930s, followed by Belgium in 1974, Germany in 1974 and France in 1988. So the United States could be considered the least "modern" of these post-industrial democracies!

Can the United States afford this? In 1963 President Kennedy was ready to go ahead at an expected cost of $11 billion. As the price index rises that amount would rise today to probably $50 billion or more. But one must remember that such a figure would include or replace some of the financial outlays already appropriated by the anti-poverty legislation passed since 1960—Medicaid, Medicare, food stamps, SSI, the 1996 Act, etc. The major point to remember is that all these efforts have fallen short–we still have 12.7%, and 37 million Americans living in poverty. The system, the government, must assume responsibility for these poor. New actions by Congress are necessary, following the many recommendations of poverty scholars such as Danziger, Gottchalk, Haveman, Corcoran, and many others.[12] Obviously a major new administrative structure would be necessary to implement such a commitment. We should go to Europe to see how they do it! We need to provide for our poor the same "fail-safe" "safety net" which Europe provides. A comprehensive assistance legislative package is necessary. And with our economic resources we can certainly afford it.

The benefits to our society would be tremendous. As scholars and analysts have reasoned for a long time, proper poor relief would have major effects on the health, educational level, family life, and morale of millions, including raising millions of poor children to a better life. Who knows–it might actually lead to the gradual clearance of our slums and ghettos and provide decent housing for all the destitute. And one scholar suggests that American business should be interested, because a successful poverty program would increase the purchasing power of the American underclass. A recent study showed that the purchasing power of households at the 10th percentile (the lowest level) is higher than that of the United States in every West European country—ranging from +21% over the United States in Belgium to +10% in the Netherlands. The West European average was +19%. These data suggest that "rulemakers in all societies should be trying to maximize the well-being of the least advantaged."[13] We can have, and should aspire to, a more fair and more socially healthy, society. And in a wealthy society we can achieve just that. At this time we certainly cannot be assured we will achieve this goal. It takes a truly concerned President and more humane and moderate Republicans (and Democrats) than we have seen in Congress recently. But we must press for such action— to create a more generous and healthy society in the United States. The great American economist and philosopher John Kenneth Galbraith wrote his famous book, The Affluent Society, in 1958, a lengthy celebration of wealth. But he included at the end a chapter on "poverty." After a careful, analytical discussion, he concludes as follows:

> "An affluent society, that is also compassionate and rational, would, no doubt, secure to all who needed it the minimum income essential for decency and comfort. . . ."
> "The myopic preoccupation with production and material investment has diverted our attention from. . . .the greater need and opportunity

for investing in persons. . . ."

"In the Unites States the survival of poverty is remarkable. We ignore it because we share with all societies at all times the capacity for not seeing what we do not wish to see. . . . In the contemporary United States (poverty) is a disgrace."[14]

This was so in 1958. Today, in 2006, poverty in America is still a disgrace. And our question to our Congressional leaders is: Is America so poor that we can't provide adequate relief for the 37 million living in poverty here? How and when will you deal with this great moral challenge of our time?

Notes

1. Harold R. Rodgers, Jr., *American Poverty in a New Era of Reform* (Armonk, NY: M.E. Sharpe, 2000), 117–127.

2. Rodgers, *American Poverty in a New Era*, 100.

3. Sheldon H. Danziger and Robert H. Haveman eds., *Understanding Poverty* (Cambridge, MA.: Harvard University Press, 2001), 188–189

4. For a striking personalized discussion of what it means to be part of the working poor in America, see Barbara Ehrenreich, *Nickel and Dimed: On Not Getting By in America* (New York: Henry Holt, 2001).

5. Rodgers, *American Poverty in a New Era*, 32.

6. One "ray of hope" emerged in the 2004 Senate deliberations on the 1996 Act reasons concerning child care. To much surprise the United States Senate voted 78 to 20 in favor of more child care. Unfortunately the House had not, by this time, endorsed this provision. But it is noteworthy that 30 Republicans joined the Senate Democrats.

7. Charles Noble, *Welfare as We Knew It: A Political History of the American Welfare State* (New York: Oxford University Press, 1997), 92.

8. Hazel Erskine, "The Polls: Government Role in Welfare", *Public Opinion Quarterly*, 39 (Summer, 1975), 259. Cited in Herbert McClosky and John Zaller, *The American Ethos: Public Attitudes Toward Capitalism and Democracy*, (Cambridge, MA: Harvard University Press, 1984), 272.

9. Warren Miller, Roy Pierce, Jacques Thomassen, Richard Herrera, Sren Holmberg, Peter Esaisson, and Bernhard Wessels, *Policy Representation in Western Democracies* (Oxford: Oxford University Press, 1999).

10. Benjamin I. Page and Robert Y. Shapiro, "Effects of Public Opinion on Policy", *American Political Science Review*, 77 (March, 1983): 175–190.

11. Russell J. Dalton, *Citizen Politics: Public Opinion and Political Practice in Advanced Industrial Democracies* (Chatham, NJ: Chatham House, 1996), 242–243.

12. For example the last chapter "Aim Anti-Poverty Agenda" in Sheldon Danziger and Peter Gottschalk, *American Unequal*, (Cambridge, MA: Harvard University Press, 1995).

13. Christopher Jencks, "Does Inequality Matter?", *Daedalus* 131, no. 1 (Winter, 2002), 49–65.

14. John K. Galbraith, *The Affluent Society* (London: Hamish Hamilton, 1960), 256–259.

Bibliography

Aberbach, Joel D., Robert D. Putnam and Bert A. Rockman. *Bureaucrats and Politicians in Western Democracies.* Cambridge, MA: Harvard University Press, 1981.

Adams, David W. *Education for Extinction: American Indians and the Boarding School Experience 1875-1928.* Lawrence, KS: University Press of Kansas, 1995.

Alexander, E. Herbert. *Financing Politics, Money, Elections and Political Reform.* Washington, DC: Congressional Quarterly Press, 1976.

Alexander, E. Herbert ed. *Comparative Political Finance in the 1980's.* New York: Cambridge University Press, 1989.

Andeweg, Rudy B. and Galen A. Irwin. *Dutch Government and Politics.* London: the Macmillan Press, 1993.

Behrendt, Christina. *At the Margins of the Welfare State. Social Assistance and the Alleviation of Poverty in Germany, Sweden, and the United Kingdom.* Burlington, VT: Ashgate Publishers, 2002.

Bellamy, Edward. *Looking Backward.* Boston: Ticknor and Company, 1888.

Berglund, Sten and Ulf Lindstrom. *The Scandinavian Party System(s).* Lund, Sweden: Studentlitt, 1978.

Berinsky, Adam J. "Silent Voices: Social Welfare Policy Opinions and Political Equality in America." *American Journal of Political Science* 46, 2 (1978), 276–287.

Bernstein, Jared. "Who's Poor? Don't Ask the Census Bureau: Why the Current Measure of Poverty Used by the Census Bureau is Obsolete" *New York Times,* (September 26, 2003), page 25.

Blom, J.C.H. and Emiel Lamberts, eds. *History of the Low Countries:.* New York: Berghahn Books, 1999.

Bochel, Hugh. *Parliament and Welfare Policy.* Aldershot, England: Dartmouth Publishing Company, 1992.

Carlson, Marybeth. "Down and Out in Rotterdam in 1700: Aspects and Functions of Poor Relief in a Dutch Town." In *The Low Countries and the New World(s): Travel, Discovery, Early Relations,* Johanna C. Prins, Bettina Brandt, Timothy Stevens, and Thomas F. Shannon, Eds.vol. 13. Lanham, MD: University Press of America, 2000.

Cray, Robert E. *Paupers and Poor Relief in New York and Its Rural Environs, 1700–1830.* Philadelphia, PA: Temple University Press, 1988.

Crowther, Margaret Anne. *The Workhouse System 1834–1929: the History of an English Social Institution.* London: Batsford Academic and Educational, 1981.

Dalton, Russell J. *Citizen Politics: Public Opinion and Political Parties in Advanced Industrial Democracies.* Chatham, NJ: Chatham House, 1996.

Danziger, Sheldon and Peter Gottschalk. *America Unequal.* Cambridge, MA: Harvard University Press, 1995.

Danziger, Sheldon H., and Robert H. Haveman eds. *Understanding Poverty.* Cambridge, MA: Harvard University Press, 2001.

Danziger, Sheldon H., Gary D. Sandefur and Daniel H. Weinberg eds. *Confronting Poverty: Prescriptions for Change.* Cambridge, MA: Harvard University Press, 1994.

Deleeck, Herman. *De Architectuur Van de Welvaartsstaat Opnieuw Bekeken.* Leuven, Belgium: Acco, 2001.

DeSchweinitz, Karl. *England's Road to Social Security: from the Statute of Laborers in 1349 to the Beveridge Report of 1942.* New York: A.S. Barnes, 1973.

DeTocqueville, Alexis. *Democracy in America.* New York: Knopf, 1945.

Edinger, Lewis J. *Politics in Germany: Attitudes and Processes.* Boston: Little, Brown, 1968.

Ehrenreich, Barbara. *Nickel and Dimed, on (not) getting by in America.* New York: Henry Holt, 2001.

Eldersveld, Samuel J. and Hanes Walton Jr. *Political Parties in American Society*. Boston: Bedford/St. Martin's, 2000.

Fine, Sidney. *Laissez-Faire and the General Welfare State: A Study of Conflict in American Thought, 1865–1901*. Ann Arbor, MI: University of Michigan Press, 1957.

Foner, Eric. *Reconstruction: America's Unfinished Revolution 1863–1877*. New York: Harper and Row, 1988.

Galbraith, John K. *The Affluent Society*. London: Hamish Hamilton, 1960.

George, Henry. *Progress and Poverty*. San Francisco: W.M. Hinton and Co., 1880.

George, Victor. *Social Security and Society*. London: Routledge and Kegan Paul, 1973.

Gilbert, Geoffrey. *World Poverty: a Reference Handbook*. Santa Barbara, CA: ABC-CLIO, 2004.

Gilens, Martin. *Why Americans Hate Welfare: Race, Media, and Politics of Anti-Poverty Policy*. Chicago: University of Chicago Press, 1999.

Gouda, Frances. *Poverty and Political Culture: The Rhetoric of Social Welfare in the Netherlands and France, 1815–1854*. Lanham, MD: Rowman & Littlefield, 1995.

Heclo, Hugh and Henrick Madsen. *Policy and Politics in Sweden: Principled Pragmatism*. Philadelphia: Temple University Press, 1987.

Himmelfarb, Gertrude. *Poverty and Compassion: the Moral Imagination of the Late Victorians*. New York: Knopf, 1991.

Hufton, Olwen, H. *The Poor of Eighteenth-Century France 1750–1789*. Oxford: Clarendon Press, 1974.

Irwin, Galen A. and Jacques Thomassen. "Issue Consensus in a Multi-Party System: Voters and Leaders in the Netherlands." *Acta Politica* 4, (October, 1975), 389–421.

Israel, Jonathan I. *The Dutch Republic: Its Rise, Greatness, and Fall, 1477–1806*. New York: Oxford University Press, 1995.

Jacobson, Gary C. *The Politics of Congressional Elections*. New York: Longman, 2000.

Jencks, Christopher. "Does Inequality Matter?" *Daedalus, Journal of the American Academy of Arts and Sciences* 131, no. 1, (Winter 2002), 49–65.

Katz, Michael P. *The Underclass Debate: View from History.* Princeton, NJ: Princeton University Press, 1993.

Katzenstein, Peter J. *Policy and Politics in West Germany: The Growth of a Semisovereign State.* Philadelphia: Temple University Press, 1987.

Keene, Karilyn and Everett C. Ladd. "Public Opinion Report." *American Enterprise,* (March/April, 1990).

Key Jr, Valdimer O. *Politics, Parties, and Pressure Groups.* New York: Crowell, 1952.

Koblik, Steven ed. *Sweden's Development from Poverty to Affluence, 1750–1970:.* Minneapolis, MN: University of Minnesota Press 1975.

Kulikoff, Allan. "The Progress of Inequality in Revolutionary Boston." *William and Mary Quarterly* 28 (July 1971), 375–393, 400–411.

Lerner, Robert, Althea K. Nagai and Stanley Rothman. *American Elites.* New Haven, CT: Yale University Press, 1996.

Luxembourg Income Study (LIS). "Relative Poverty Rates for the Total Population, Children and the Elderly." January 2006. http://www.lisproject.org/keyfigures/povertytable.htm (accessed August 21, 2006).

Matthews, Donald R. *U.S. Senators and Their World.* New York: Norton, 1973.

Mayhew, David. *Divided We Govern: Party Control, Lawmaking, and Investigations, 1946–1990.* New Haven: Yale University Press, 1991.

McCloskey, Herbert and John Zaller. *The American Ethos: Public Attitudes Toward Capitalism and Democracy.* Cambridge, MA: Harvard University Press, 1984.

Meisel, James H. *The Myth of the Ruling Class: Gaetano Mosca and the "Elite."* Ann Arbor, MI: University of Michigan Press, 1962.

Michels, Roberto. *Political Parties: a Sociological Study of the Oligarchical Tendencies of Modern Democracy.* New York: Dover Publications, 1959.

Miller, Nathan. *FDR An Intimate History.* Lanham, MD: Madison Books, 1983.

Miller, Warren E., Roy Pierce, Jacques Thomassen, Richard Herrera, Soren Holmberg, Peter Esaiasson and Bernhard Wessels. *Policy Representation in Western Democracies.* New York: Oxford University Press, 1999.

Mitchell, Allan. *The Divided Path: The German Influence on Social Reform in France After 1870.* Chapel Hill, NC: University of North Carolina Press, 1991.

Mosca, Gaetano. *The Ruling Class.* New York: McGraw Hill, 1939.

Nash, Gary B. *The Urban Crucible: the Northern Seaports and the Origins of the American Revolution.* Cambridge, MA: Harvard University Press, 1986.

Newton, Gerald. *The Netherlands: An Historical and Cultural Survey 1795-1977.* Boulder, CO: Westview Press, 1978.

New York Times, August 27, 2004.

New York Times, September 5, 2002.

Noble, Charles. *Welfare as We Knew It: a Political History of the American Welfare State.* New York: Oxford University Press, 1997.

Nordstrom, Byron J. *Scandinavia Since 1500.* Minneapolis, MN: University of Minnesota Press, 2000.

Page, Benjamin I. and Robert Y. Shapiro. *The Rational Public: Fifty Years of Trends in Americans Policy Preferences.* Chicago: University of Chicago Press, 1992.

Page, Benjamin I. and Robert Y. Shapiro. "Effects of Public Opinion on Policy." *American Political Science Review* 77 (March 1983), 175–190.

Pareto, Vilfredo. *Sociological Writings.* New York: Praeger, 1966.

Phillips, Kevin P. *Wealth and Democracy: A Political History of the American Rich.* New York: Broadway Books, 2002.

Pierce, Roy. *French Politics and Political Institutions.* New York: Harper and Row, 1968.

Poen, Monte M. *Harry S. Truman Versus the Medical Lobby: the Genesis of Medicare.* Columbia, MO: University of Missouri Press, 1979.

Pomper, Gerald M., E.J. Dionne Jr., William G. Mayer, Marjorie Randon Hershey, Kathleen A. Frankovic, Monika L. McDermott, Anthony Corrado, Paul S. Herrnson and Wilson Carey McWilliams. *The Election of 2000: Reports and Interpretations.* New York: Chatham House Publishers, 2001.

Putnam, Robert D. *The Comparative Study of Political Elites.* Englewood Cliffs, NJ: Prentice Hall, 1976.

Rockman, Seth. *Welfare Reform in the Early Republic: a Brief History with Documents.* Boston: Bedford/St. Martin's, 2003.

Rodgers, Harrell R. Jr. *American Poverty in a New Era of Reform.* Armonk, NY: M.E. Sharpe, 2000.

Sachs, Jeffrey D. *The End of Poverty: Economic Possibilities for Our Time.* New York: Penguin Press, 2005.

Schama, Simon. *The Embarrassment of Riches: An Interpretation of Dutch Culture in the Golden Age.* New York: Knopf, 1987.

Schattschneider, Elmer E. *The Semisovereign People: a Realist's View of Democracy in America.* Hinsdale, IL: Dryden Press, 1960.

Schut, J.M.W., J.C. Vrooman, and P.T. de Beer. *On Worlds of Welfare: Institutions and their Effects in Eleven Welfare States.* The Hague, the Netherlands: Social and Cultural Planning Office of the Netherlands, 2001.

Skocpol, Theda. *Social Policy in the United States: Future Possibilities in Historical Perspective.* Princeton, NJ: Princeton University Press, 1995.

Smeeding, Timothy. "Poor People in Rich Nations: The United States in Comparative Perspective." *The Journal of Economic Perspectives* 20, no. 1, (Winter 2006), 69–90.

Smith, Adam. *An Inquiry into the Nature and Causes of the Wealth of Nations.* London: W. Strahan and T. Cadell, 1776.

Sorensen, Theodore C. *Kennedy.* New York: Harper and Row, 1965.

Stanley, Harold W. and Richard G. Niemi. *Vital Statistics on American Politics.* Washington, DC Congressional Quarterly Press 1995.

Statistical Abstract of the United States. Unemployment outlook, 2000.

Stephens, John D. *The Transition from Capitalism to Socialism.* Urbana, IL: University of Illinois Press, 1986.

Tournier, Eric. *Economie et Société Françaises Depuis 1973.* Paris: Nathan, 1999.

Uhr, Carl G. Sweden's Social Security: an Appraisal of its Economic Impact in the Postwar Period. Washington, DC: U.S. Department of Health, Education, and Welfare, Social Security Administration, Office of Research and Statistics; U.S. Government. Printing Office 1966.

United States Census Bureau. "Historical Poverty Tables", March 2006. http://www.census.gov/hhes/www/poverty/histpov/hstpov2.html (accessed August 21, 2006).

Van Loo, L. Frank. *Arm in Nederland, 1815–1900.* Meppel, the Netherlands: Boom, 1992.

Verba, Sidney. "Participation and Participatory Equality: Why Do We Want It? Why Might We Not?" Paper presented at the University of Michigan, April 10, 2003.

Verba, Sidney and Gary R. Orrin. *Equality in America: The View from the Top.* Cambridge, MA: Harvard University Press, 1985.

Verba, Sidney and Norman H. Nie. *Participation in America.* New York: Harper, 1972.

Verba, Sidney and Steven Kelman. *Elites and the Idea of Equality: a comparison of Japan, Sweden, and the United States.* Cambridge, MA: Harvard University Press, 1987.

Verba, Sidney, Kay Lehman Schlozman and Henry E. Brady. *Voice and Equality: Civic Voluntarism in American Politics.* Cambridge, MA: Harvard University Press, 1995.

Whiteley, Paul, Patrick Seyd and Jeremy Richardson. *True Blues: The Politics of Conservative Party Membership.* Oxford: Clarendon Press, 1994.

Wilentz, Sean. "America's Lost Equalitarian Tradition." *Daedalus Journal of the American Academy of Arts and Sciences* (Winter 2002), Vol. 131, No. 1, 66–80.

Yesilada, Birol ed. *Comparative Political Parties and Party Elites: Essays in Honor of Samuel J. Eldersveld:.* Ann Arbor, MI: University of Michigan Press 1999.

Index

163

About the Author

Samuel J. Eldersveld is professor emeritus of political science at the University of Michigan. He has taught at Michigan since 1946 when he received his doctorate at that university. He was chair of the department from 1964 to 1970, leading the development and expansion of the department to its recognition as one of the top ranked departments in the country. He was also active in politics and successfully ran for mayor of Ann Arbor in 1957, serving until 1959. His major fields of study have been American political parties, public opinion, and elections; and comparative politics focussing particularly on the Netherlands, India and recently, China. He has written, or participated in writing, over twenty books which were studies of the politics of these systems. In 1964 he received the Woodrow Wilson Award for the best book in American politics. Much of his comparative work dealt with political elites, national and local. He has conducted studies of local government and local political leadership, alone or in collaboration with other scholars, in the United States, the Netherlands, Sweden, India, Taiwan, and recently mainland China. In 1995 he published Local Elites in Western Democracies (with Swedish and Dutch coauthors). He also published in 1995 a study of Ann Arbor politics – Party Conflicts and Community Development. Earlier, in 1978, he published Citizens and Politics: Mass Political Behavior in India (with an Indian coauthor). His most recent article was a comparison of popular support for economic reform by the public and local elites of China and India in the journal Comparative Political Studies (April 2000). His last publication was Support for Economic and Political Change in the China Countryside. An Empirical Study of Cadres and Villagers in Four Counties 1990, and 1996, coauthored with a Chinese scholar.